Spelling Counts

Sounds and Patterns for English Language Learners

Janet Giannotti

Ann Arbor

THE UNIVERSITY OF MICHIGAN PRESS

Published in the United States of America
The University of Michigan Press
Manufactured in the United States of America

∞ Printed on acid-free paper

ISBN-13: 978-0-472-03347-8

2012 2011 2010 2009 4 3 2 1

Contents

Information for Teachers and Students

Spelling Counts is a workbook that guides ESL students through the basics of spelling by listening for sounds and by examining patterns in the vowel and consonant systems of written English. It is intended for adult or secondary school students at the low-intermediate level or higher and is appropriate for mixed-level classes. It may be used in high schools, in community college academic and community-based programs, in adult education classes, and in intensive English programs. Students who benefit most from the book may speak quite fluently and should know a fair amount of vocabulary. They may not, however, be completely familiar with the sound/symbol correspondences of English.

Spelling Counts is designed to be flexible in its use in that it can be an add-on text to a reading, vocabulary, grammar, pronunciation, or integrated skills class, or it can be the focal point of a spelling class, especially if supplemented with reading material that can be used as a resource for exemplars. It is intended for classroom use, as it relies on a teacher with native-speaker pronunciation, and it includes a small amount of material to be used for independent study (i.e., homework). *It is not meant to be a book that can be handed to a student who has trouble with spelling.* It is, instead, a course text for teacher-led instruction. As such, the text contains a Teacher's Script located at the end of the book from which teachers read. *No audio is provided.* The approach in *Spelling Counts* works for a wide variety of learners as it takes an academic approach yet moves slowly and methodically through the sound-letter correspondences of English. Students are asked to analyze examples and complete descriptions of spelling patterns in each lesson. Teachers can work through these descriptions, called Pattern Discoveries, with students.

Spelling Counts derives some of its approach from the field of word study, a method that asks learners to investigate patterns and understand phonics rather than memorize lists of unrelated words. Thus students learn to spell English rather than learning to spell the words of English. This may be a fine distinction, but students should have, as their goal, the ability to hear an unfamiliar word, write it down, and then find it in the dictionary. Another goal is for students to hear a term or name in a lecture and, again, be able to write it, approximating correct spelling, and later be able to match the name or term to a reference in a textbook. If a student in a history class hears *squire* and writes *skwair,* that student will be unsuccessful with a dictionary, the course text, and in a testing situation. Once students learn that [kwai] is most often represented with *qui* (*quite, quiet, squire, require*), they have a key to success.

Spelling Counts moves through the first three stages of word study: from letter name spelling for short vowel sounds to within-word patterns for long vowels, and finally to syllables and affixes (also known as syllable juncture) for doubling and *e*-drop patterns. Teachers may find useful supplemental materials by searching for these stages on the Internet.

In addition to this focus on seeing and relying on patterns in spelling, *Spelling Counts* helps students learn many words that do not follow patterns. Therefore, each lesson also introduces three to six "must spell" words, which are recycled through the unit. These words are generally referred to as "sight words," and that is the label they are given here. The thinking is that these words just "look right" or "look wrong" to a native speaker, and everyone is expected to be able to spell them correctly, even though they often do not follow the basic rules covered in the material. With the inclusion of these sight words, by using *Spelling Counts*, students will gain confidence in their ability to spell not only unknown words like *clutch* and *gobble*, but also familiar words that they may say every day, like *Tuesday* or *once*.

One important point to keep in mind is that spelling instruction must be administered in small doses. Therefore, *Spelling Counts* presents many short lessons. Teachers may work on one or more lessons in a given class period, and may recycle material and create extra quizzes from the exemplars in the textbook as needed.

Another important point to keep in mind is that spelling instruction requires students to recycle everything and asks teachers to never mistake understanding nods and apparent lightbulbs-over-heads for acquisition. Teachers should check students' accuracy often, on exercises presented in the book as well as on additional quizzes. If students have invented their own spelling systems, it is essential that they start at the very beginning to rebuild, erase the flaws, and fill in the gaps in their personal knowledge. Teachers are encouraged to move as quickly as necessary through the first pages of the book, slowing down when students begin to make too many errors. Students will start by spelling *bit* and *twin*, move into an understanding of why *hopping* has a double *p* while *hoping* has one, distinguish homophones like *stairs* and *stares*, add endings to create longer words like *hopefully*, and spell compound words like *nightlife*.

An answer key can be found online at www.press.umich.edu/esl/.

Unit 1

Introduction to Short Vowels

■ Unit 1 Overview

FIVE VOWELS

Read this passage with your teacher. Notice the words and names in **bold.**

> English "nursery rhymes," or poems for children, often feature a man named "**Jack**." There is Jack who **fell** down a **hill** with **his** friend **Jill**. **Then** we have **Jack** who was quick and **jumped** over a candle **stick.** We also have **Jack Sprat**, who couldn't eat **fat**. And finally, we have little **Jack** Horner, who pulled a **plum** out of a pie with his **thumb**. No one knows why we use the name **Jack** in these rhymes and not **Tom** or **Bob**!

Study the words and names from the reading, and complete the Pattern Discovery on page 2.

hill Jill stick	fell then	Jack Sprat fat	jump plum thumb	Tom Bob

Pattern Discovery

How many vowels does each word contain? ____
These are the five short vowels in English. If a one-syllable word contains a short vowel, there is ____ vowel in the word.
Circle the vowel in each word.

Look at this chart that shows where these vowel sounds are produced in the mouth.

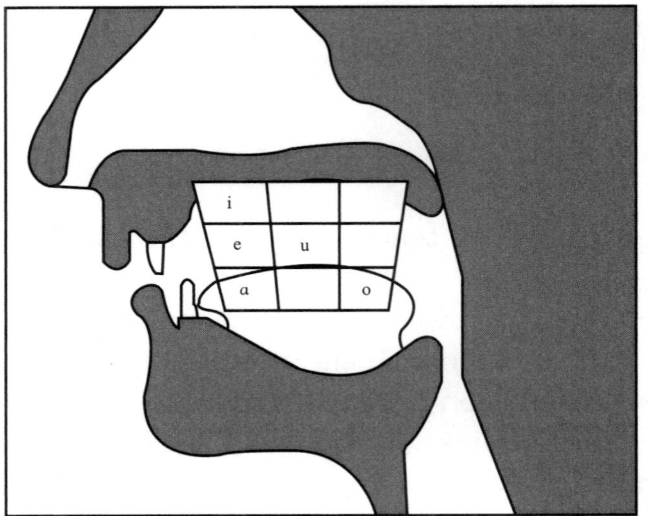

Listen and Write

Listen as your teacher pronounces these short-vowel words. Fill in the missing letter. Study the description of each vowel. (*Reminder for the teacher:* Please read from the Teacher's Script beginning on page 131.)

1. h__ll st__ck — Short *i* is a high front vowel.
2. f__ll th__n — Short *e* is a mid front vowel.
3. J__ck f__t — Short *a* is a low front vowel.
4. j__mp pl__m — Short *u* is a mid vowel.
5. T__m B__b — Short *o* is a low back vowel.

Application

Find nursery rhymes about people named Jack on the Internet. Notice the short-vowel words in the rhymes.

Lesson 1: Short *i*

Words

Pronounce these words with your teacher.

bit	kit	chip	rip	chin	skin	kick	stick
fit	lit	dip	skip	fin	spin	lick	tick
grit	slit	hip	trip	grin	twin	pick	trick
hit	wit	lip	zip	pin	win	sick	wick

Pronunciation Tip

Short *i* is a high front vowel. Don't drop your chin when you say short *i*.

Pattern Review

If a one-syllable word contains a short vowel, there is ____ vowel in the word. This means that short-vowel words have ____ vowel per syllable.

Pattern Discovery 1

At the end of a short-vowel word, the sound [k] is spelled -____.

Listening Discrimination 1

Circle the words you hear. (*Reminder for the teacher:* Please read from the Teacher's Script beginning on page 131.)

1. grit	grip	5. chin	tin
2. kick	kit	6. wit	wick
3. slip	slit	7. spin	pin
4. slit	slick	8. trick	chick

Listen and Write 1

Listen and fill in the missing consonants.

1. bi_____	5. chi_____	9. _____it
2. gri_____	6. spi_____	10. _____ip
3. hi_____	7. li_____	11. _____in
4. tri_____	8. sti_____	12. _____ick

Sight Words

Study the spelling of these words, and then copy each word three times.

weekend	Saturday	Sunday

weekend ________________ ________________ ________________

Saturday ________________ ________________ ________________

Sunday ________________ ________________ ________________

Pattern Discovery 2

Names of days begin with capital / small (circle one) letters.

Choose and Write

Use the short *i* words in the box to complete the sentences.

chip	dip	fit	grin	kick	win

1. You have to ____________ the ball.
2. A ____________ is a wide smile.
3. She ate some ____________ on a ____________.
4. Did they ____________ the game?
5. My old shoes don't ____________.

Listen and Write 2

Write the short *i* words you hear.

1. ____________	4. ____________	7. ____________
2. ____________	5. ____________	8. ____________
3. ____________	6. ____________	9. ____________

Sight Word Practice

Use the words in the box to complete the sentences.

weekend	Saturday	Sunday

1. The day after Friday is ________________.
2. ________________ is before Monday.
3. The party will be on the ________________.
4. Will the party be on ________________ or ________________?

Listening Discrimination 2

Circle the word you hear.

1. lip	lick	lit	4. zip	chip	ship
2. tin	tip	tick	5. slip	rip	lip
3. trick	trip	chip	6. sick	sit	sip

Listen and Write 3

Listen and fill in the short *i* words and sight words from this lesson.

1. She ____________ her ____________.
2. He was ____________ on ________________.
3. We take a ____________ every ________________.
4. Did you ____________ the paper?
5. Don't ____________ the ball.

■ Lesson 2: Short *i*

Words

Pronounce these words and names with your teacher.

brick	brim	trim	big	bid	lid
click	dim	Jim	dig	did	mid
Rick	him	Kim	pig	hid	rid
Nick	rim	Tim	wig	kid	Sid
bricks	brims	whims	figs	grids	lids
clicks	rims		wigs	kids	

Pronunciation Tip

Combinations like *br-*, *fl-*, and *gr-* are called **consonant blends.** Don't insert a vowel sound between the two consonants in a blend.

Pattern Review 1

Short-vowel words have ____ vowel per syllable.

Pattern Review 2

At the end of a short-vowel word, the sound [k] is spelled -____.

Pattern Discovery

Add -____ to change a noun from singular to plural.

Listening Discrimination

Circle the words you hear.

1. flit	flick	5. clicks	clips
2. slip	slit	6. brick	Rick
3. chip	trip	7. hid	hits
4. trick	chick	8. licks	lids

Listen and Write 1

Listen and fill in the missing consonants.

1. bri____
2. Ji____
3. bi____
4. ____id
5. ____icks
6. ____ims
7. pi____
8. li____
9. whi____

Sight Words

Study the spelling of these words, and use them to complete the sentences.

weekday	Monday	Tuesday	tomorrow

1. ________________ comes before ________________.
2. Saturday is on the weekend, but ________________ is a ________________.
3. On ________________, I said, "________________ is Tuesday."

Pattern Review 3

Names of days begin with capital / small letters (circle one).

Choose and Write

Use the words and names in the box to complete the sentences. Use each word one time. Various combinations work.

did	Kim	Rick	tomorrow	Tuesday
kids	Monday	Tim	trim	twins

1. ____________ is going to New York ____________.
2. ____________ and Jim are ____________.
3. The ____________ played last ____________.
4. What ____________ you do on ____________?
5. ____________ is going to ____________ her hair.

Add an Ending

Add *-s* to these nouns to change them to plural. Write the plural nouns on the lines. Pronounce the words after you write them.

1. kit ____________
2. slit ____________
3. chip ____________
4. hip ____________
5. lip ____________
6. rip ____________
7. trip ____________
8. chin ____________
9. grin ____________
10. pin ____________
11. twin ____________
12. stick ____________
13. trick ____________
14. brick ____________
15. brim ____________
16. rim ____________
17. pig ____________
18. wig ____________
19. bid ____________
20. lid ____________
21. kid ____________

Listen and Write 2

Write the plural nouns you hear.

1. ____________
2. ____________
3. ____________
4. ____________
5. ____________
6. ____________
7. ____________
8. ____________
9. ____________

Listen and Write 3

Listen and fill in the short *i* words and sight words from this lesson.

1. ____________ bought the bricks last ________________.
2. ____________ the right mouse button or ____________ the space bar.
3. ____________ the hat have a wide ____________?
4. ____________ put the ____________ on the pot to make it boil.
5. The road crews never ____________ on a ________________.
6. ____________ will trim the bushes ________________.

■ Lesson 3: Short *u*

Words

Pronounce these words with your teacher.

pub	bug	buck	gum	fun	but	fudge
rub	dug	luck	hum	run	shut	budge
scrub	hug	struck	rum	stun	strut	grudge
tubs	rugs	trucks	sums	guns	cuts	judges

Pronunciation Tip

Short *u* is a mid vowel. Drop your jaw a little when you say short *u*.

Pattern Review 1

At the end of a short-vowel word, the sound [k] is spelled -____.

Pattern Review 2

Add -____ to make a noun plural.

Pattern Discovery

After a short vowel, the sound [ǰ] is spelled with three letters. They are -____.

Listening Discrimination 1

Circle the words you hear.

1. stub	scrub	4. tuck	truck
2. hug	chug	5. grudge	judge
3. sub	shrug	6. truck	chuck

Find the Base Form

Write the singular form of the nouns.

1. cubs ____________	3. bucks ____________	5. huts ____________
2. hugs ____________	4. judges ____________	6. grudges ____________

Listen and Write 1

Listen and fill in the missing consonants.

1. ____ut	4. chu____	7. ____un
2. ____un	5. fu____	8. ____ut
3. ____udge	6. scru____	9. ____ub

Sight Words

Study the spelling of these days, and use them to complete the sentences.

Wednesday	Thursday	Friday

1. Thursday comes after ____________________ but before ____________________.
2. ____________________ is between Wednesday and ____________________.
3. Friday comes after ____________________ and ____________________.
4. She has to work on Friday, but not on ____________________ or ____________________.

Choose and Write

Use the short *u* words in the box to complete the sentences.

fudge	judge	shut	gum	rug	tub

1. Please ____________ the door.
2. Don't chew ____________ in pronunciation class.
3. I bought ____________ at the candy shop.
4. The ____________ is on the floor.
5. Is there a ____________ in the bathroom?
6. He spoke to the ____________ in court.

Listen and Write 2

Write the short *u* words you hear.

1. ____________
2. ____________
3. ____________
4. ____________
5. ____________
6. ____________
7. ____________
8. ____________
9. ____________

Listening Discrimination 2

Circle the words you hear.

1.	Tuesday	Wednesday	Thursday
2.	scrub	shrub	shrubs
3.	shuck	trucks	chuck
4.	Tuesday	Wednesday	Thursday
5.	bud	buds	budge
6.	stuck	stub	struck

Listen and Write 3

Listen and fill in the short *u* words and sight words from this lesson.

1. We had ____________ last ____________.
2. He ____________ a hole in the ____________ in front of the little ____________.
3. The ____________ was ____________. It wouldn't ____________.
4. The shop sells dried fruit, ____________, and ____________.
5. I still have my ticket ____________ from the movie I saw on ____________.
6. They went to a ____________ last ____________.
7. That ____________ ____________ to the bottom of my shoe.
8. If the player can't ____________, they'll send in a ____________.

■ Lesson 4: Short *i* and Short *u* in Contrast

Words

Pronounce these words with your teacher.

bin	bun	lick	luck	ditch	clutch
fin	fun	pick	puck	hitch	crutch
pin	pun	stick	stuck	pitch	Dutch
spin	spun	trick	truck	witch	hutch

Pronunciation Tip

Pairs of words like *bin* and *bun* are called **minimal pairs** because they differ in only one sound. Say some of the minimal pairs from the list above. Notice the difference between short *i* and short *u*.

Pattern Review 1

Short-vowel words have ____ vowel per syllable.

Pattern Review 2

At the end of a short-vowel word, the sound [k] is spelled -____.

Pattern Discovery

After a short-vowel word, the sound [č] is spelled with three letters. They are -_____.

Now study these words. Do they follow the pattern?

rich	sandwich	which	much	such

Pattern Exception

The [č] sound is usually spelled -____ after a short vowel. However, there are five exceptions to this pattern. They are ____________, ____________, ____________, ____________, and ____________.

Listening Discrimination

Circle the words you hear.

1. shin	chin	5. scrub	shrub
2. hum	him	6. dish	ditch
3. jug	jig	7. trick	truck
4. hut	hutch	8. chuck	chick

Listen and Write 1

Listen and fill in the missing vowels.

1. r__b	5. fl__p	9. tw__st
2. sp__n	6. dr__p	10. r__st
3. st__ck	7. h__tch	11. r__sh
4. m__g	8. p__tch	12. sw__ft

Sight Words

Study the days and their abbreviations, and use them to complete the sentences.

Monday = Mon.	Tuesday = Tues.	Wednesday = Wed.	Thursday = Thurs.

1. The abbreviation for ____________________ is Mon.
2. The abbreviation for Tuesday is _____________.
3. The abbreviation for ____________________ is Wed.
4. The abbreviation for Thursday is _____________.
5. Mon. is the abbreviation for ____________________.
6. _____________ is the abbreviation for ____________________.
7. _____________ is the abbreviation for ____________________.
8. _____________ is the abbreviation for ____________________.

Choose and Write

Use the words in the box to complete the sentences.

big	ditch	pin	stuck
bugs	dug	rug	truck
clutch	fix	six	tub

1. There is a ____________ ____________ on the floor.
2. The crew ____________ a ____________ near the road.
3. He ____________ a ____________ into the shirt.
4. The ____________ has a broken ____________ that he needs to ____________.
5. ____________ ____________ floated in the ____________ of water.

Listen and Write 2

Write the words you hear.

1. ____________
2. ____________
3. ____________
4. ____________
5. ____________
6. ____________
7. ____________
8. ____________
9. ____________

Listen and Write 3

Listen and fill in the short *u* and short *i* words.

Last year, ____________ bought a ____________ ____________. It was ____________ years old, ____________ it was in good condition. It had a ____________ on the back so he could pull his boat. Now ____________ is having some bad ____________ with his ____________. First, he had to replace the ____________ because he couldn't ____________ the gears. Then the ____________ got ____________ in some ____________ and a ____________ cap fell off the wheel. Last night, someone ____________ the truck in a parking lot. Now ____________ wonders what ____________ going to happen next.

Lesson 5: Short *i* and Short *u* in Contrast

Words

Pronounce these words with your teacher.

big	bridge	stiff	bill	hiss
dig	ridge	cliff	hill	kiss
pig	fridge	whiff	kill	miss
twig			pill	bliss
bug	budge	cuff	dull	cuss
dug	fudge	fluff	gull	muss
rug	grudge	huff	hull	fuss
plug	judge	stuff	lull	truss

Pattern Review 1

After a short vowel, the sound [ǰ] is spelled -____.

Pattern Review 2

Short-vowel words have ____ vowel per syllable.

Pattern Exception

Short-vowel words that end with the sound [ǰ] end with a silent ____.

Pattern Discovery

At the end of a short-vowel syllable, the sounds [f], [l], or [s] are most often written -____, -____, and -____.

Listen and Write 1

Listen and fill in the missing letter or letters.

1. ____idge
2. ____iff
3. ____iss
4. ____uff
5. twi____
6. bu____
7. pu____
8. hi____
9. bri____
10. hu____
11. sti____
12. ju____

Listen and Write 2

Listen and fill in the missing vowels.

1. d__g
2. pl__g
3. gr__dge
4. cl_ff
5. p__ff
6. br__dge
7. g__ll
8. m__ss

Add an Ending

Add -*s* to these nouns to change them to plural. Write the plural nouns on the lines.

1. bridge ____________
2. cliff ____________
3. hill ____________
4. judge ____________
5. cuff ____________
6. gull ____________

Pattern Review 3

Add -____ to change a noun from singular to plural.

Sight Words

Study the days and their abbreviations, and use them to complete the sentences.

Friday = Fri.	Saturday = Sat.	Sunday = Sun.

1. The abbreviation for ________________ is Fri.
2. The abbreviation for Saturday is ____________.
3. The abbreviation for ________________ is Sun.
4. Sat. is the abbreviation for ________________.
5. ____________ is the abbreviation for ________________.
6. ____________ is the abbreviation for ________________.
7. ____________ is the abbreviation for ________________.

Choose and Write

Use the words in the box to complete the sentences.

bliss	fridge	pills
bug	fuss	twig
cuff	grudge	whiff

1. A ____________ is a small stick or branch.
2. A ____________ is an insect.
3. If you hold a ____________, you don't forgive someone.
4. Your ____________ is in your kitchen.
5. A ____________ is a smell.
6. I took some ____________ when I was sick.
7. If you make a ____________, you complain.
8. ____________ is great happiness.
9. Your ____________ is at the end of your sleeve.

Find the Base Form

Write the singular form of the nouns.

1. plugs ____________
2. judges ____________
3. puffs ____________
4. pills ____________
5. ridges ____________
6. twigs ____________
7. grudges ____________
8. whiffs ____________
9. ridges ____________

Listen and Write 3

Write the words you hear.

1. ____________
2. ____________
3. ____________
4. ____________
5. ____________
6. ____________
7. ____________
8. ____________
9. ____________

■ Unit 1 Review Pages

PATTERN RECAP

There are ____ short vowels.
The short vowels can be placed on a vowel chart that looks like this:

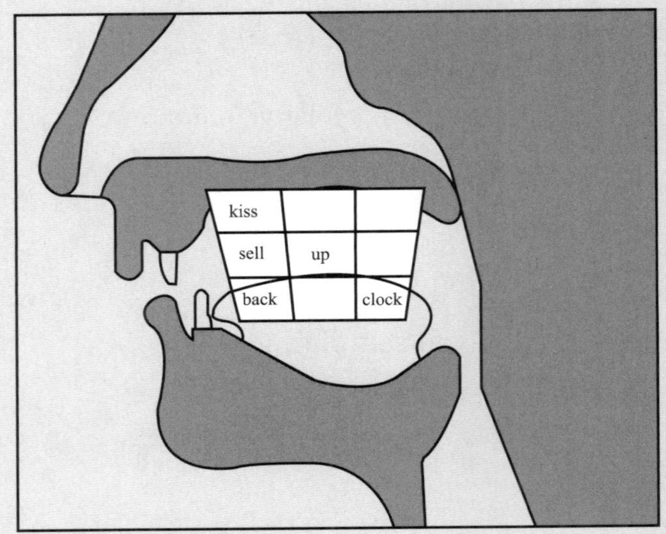

1. Short-vowel words have ____ vowel per syllable.
   - ■ Pattern exception: Words ending with the [ǰ] sound end with *-dge.*
2. At the end of a short-vowel syllable, we write -____ to spell the sound [k].
3. At the end of a short-vowel syllable, we write -____ to spell the sound [ǰ].
4. At the end of a short-vowel syllable, we write -____ to spell the sound [č].
   - ■ Pattern exception: Five common words do not follow this pattern. They are:

     ____________ ____________ ____________

     ____________ ____________
5. At the end of a short-vowel word, we write -____ to spell the sound [f].
6. At the end of a short-vowel word, we write -____ to spell the sound [l].
7. At the end of a short-vowel word, we usually write -____ to spell the sound [s].
8. We usually add -____ to make a noun plural.

Listen and Write 1

Write the words you hear.

1. ________	9. ________	17. ________
2. ________	10. ________	18. ________
3. ________	11. ________	19. ________
4. ________	12. ________	20. ________
5. ________	13. ________	21. ________
6. ________	14. ________	22. ________
7. ________	15. ________	23. ________
8. ________	16. ________	24. ________

Sight Word Review

Fill in the abbreviation for each day.

Sunday		Thursday	
Monday		Friday	
Tuesday		Saturday	
Wednesday			

Sight Word Review

Fill in the missing words and days.

1. The two weekend days are ________ and Sunday.
2. Monday and ________ are the first two weekdays.
3. ________ is the last ________ before the weekend.
4. ________ comes after Monday and before ________.
5. Saturday and ________ are on the ________.
6. ________ is the day before Friday.
7. ________ comes after Sunday and before ________.

Add an Ending

Change each noun to plural. Write the plural nouns on the lines.

1. duck ____________ 4. cuff ____________ 7. judge ____________
2. brim ____________ 5. bridge ____________ 8. truck ____________
3. stick ____________ 6. bill ____________ 9. cliff ____________

Listen and Write 2

Listen and fill in the short *i,* short *u,* and sight words from Unit 1.

Rose had a busy week. On ________________, she went grocery shopping. Her ____________ was empty and she needed to ____________ it up. On ________________, Rose had an appointment with her hairdresser, ____________. Rose wanted Kim to ____________ her hair. Kim ____________ a good job. On ________________, Rose took a little ____________. She visited her brother ____________. Tim had been ____________, but he was feeling better. Rose gave Tim a ____________ and a ____________ before she left his house. Tim doesn't like it when Rose makes a ____________ over him. On ________________, Rose worked in her yard. She had to ____________ a little ____________ at the edge of the garden, ____________ the ____________, and ____________ up some ____________ that blew over in a storm. Today is ________________. Rose is going to ____________ some errands today. She is hoping to get some rest on the ________________.

Spelling Names

Many English surnames follow common spelling patterns. Tell what you know about the spelling of these common names. What vowel appears in the first syllable? What consonant patterns do you see?

1. Mitchell 5. Williams 9. Hutchinson
2. Miller 6. Hill 10. Gifford
3. Russell 7. Richards 11. Phillips
4. Gibson 8. Cummings 12. Hunter

Word Search Puzzle

There are 12 short *i* and short *u* words in this puzzle. They all appear horizontally; look from left to right. Circle the words, write them at the bottom of the page, and tell at least one fact that you know about each word. One has been done for you as an example.

i	p	i	t	c	h	i	l	u
u	i	r	g	r	u	d	g	e
s	t	u	f	f	f	b	i	t
c	i	b	i	l	l	s	p	p
c	l	u	t	c	h	h	u	l
u	s	s	f	u	s	s	i	l
c	l	u	b	s	s	p	i	g
s	k	u	l	l	s	s	i	l
r	p	i	f	c	l	i	c	k
t	r	u	c	k	s	u	f	l

Example: pitch

Pitch has a short *i*. It ends with the sound [č], which is spelled *-tch*.

1. ____________
2. ____________
3. ____________
4. ____________
5. ____________
6. ____________
7. ____________
8. ____________
9. ____________
10. ____________
11. ____________

Unit 2

More Short Vowels

■ Unit 2 Overview

HEARING SYLLABLES

Read this passage with your teacher. Notice the words and names in **bold**.

> Sheldon "Shel" Silverstein (1930–1999) was a poet and songwriter. Some of Shel Silverstein's **best**-known poems for children were published in several books including *A Light in the Attic, Where the Sidewalk* ***Ends,*** and *Falling* ***Up***. Silverstein's silly and imaginative poems have interesting rhymes and funny stories. Some of the poems have **short** titles like "Messy Room," "**Sick**," or "**Smart**."

Study these words, and complete the Pattern Review.

best	Ends	Up	short	Sick	Smart

Pattern Review 1

Short-vowel words have ____ vowel per syllable.

Now read the passage again, noting the words in bold.

> Sheldon "Shel" Silverstein (1930–1999) was a poet and songwriter. Some of Shel Silverstein's best-known poems for **children** were published in several books including *A Light in the **Attic**, Where the Sidewalk Ends,* and ***Falling** Up*. Silverstein's **silly** and imaginative poems have interesting rhymes and **funny** stories. Most of the poems have short titles like "**Messy** Room," "Sick," or "Smart."

These short-vowel words have two syllables. Pronounce these words with your teacher.

children	Attic	Falling	silly	funny	Messy

Pronunciation Tip

Make a fist with your thumb up, and hold it below your chin. Don't touch your chin. As you pronounce words, your chin will touch your thumb once per syllable.

Pattern Review 2

When short-vowel words have two or more syllables, they still have ____ vowel per ___________. Circle two vowels in each of the words in the box.

Application

Find some poems written by Shel Silverstein by looking on the Internet or at your local library. Look for short-vowel words in his poems.

■ Lesson 6: Short *a*

Words

Pronounce these words with your teacher.

cash	back	batch	brass
dash	crack	catch	class
rash	pack	match	mass
splash	track	scratch	pass

Pronunciation Tip

Short *a* is a low front vowel. Try smiling when you pronounce short *a*.

Pattern Discovery

The sound [š] is spelled - ____.

Pattern Review

At the end of a short-vowel syllable, the sound [k] is spelled - ____.
At the end of a short-vowel syllable, the sound [č] is spelled - ____.
At the end of a short-vowel syllable, and the sound [s] is spelled - ____.

Listen and Write 1

Listen and fill in the missing consonants.

1. la____
2. la____
3. ma____
4. ma____
5. pa____
6. pa____
7. pa____
8. tra____
9. ____ack
10. ____ash
11. ____ass
12. ____atch

Listening Discrimination

Pronounce these short *a* words with your teacher. After each word, write the number of syllables on the line. The words have one or two syllables.

1. packer ____
2. patch ____
3. scratch ____
4. passing ____
5. racks ____
6. splashing ____
7. tracks ____
8. cash ____
9. cracker ____

Sight Words

Study the spelling of these numbers, and use them to complete the sentences.

one	two	three	four	five	six

1. There is ____________ day between Tuesday and Thursday, but there are ____________ weekdays.
2. There are ____________ days between Monday and Saturday and ____________ days between Sunday and Thursday.
3. There are ____________ weekdays and ____________ days on the weekend.
4. If he works ____________ days a week, he has only one day off.

Choose and Write

Use the short *a* words in the box to complete the sentences.

batch	bath	cat	class	Jack	pass	scratch

1. My ____________ doesn't ____________.
2. ____________ gave the baby a ____________.
3. She needs to ____________ this ____________.
4. She baked a ____________ of cookies.

Listen and Write 2

Write the short *a* words you hear.

1. ____________
2. ____________
3. ____________
4. ____________
5. ____________
6. ____________
7. ____________
8. ____________

Listening Discrimination 1

Pronounce these words and names with your teacher. After each word, write the number of syllables on the line. The words have one or two syllables.

1. attic ____
2. short ____
3. messy ____
4. ends ____
5. children ____
6. up ____
7. best ____
8. sick ____
9. silly ____

Listening Discrimination 2

Circle the words you hear.

1. pick pack puck
2. tuck tack tick
3. mass muss miss
4. hatch hitch hutch
5. clack click cluck
6. hash hatch hush

Listen and Write 3

Write the short *i*, short *u*, and short *a* words you hear.

1. ____________
2. ____________
3. ____________
4. ____________
5. ____________
6. ____________
7. ____________
8. ____________

Lesson 7: Short *o*

Words

Pronounce these words with your teacher.

knob	dock	hop	hot
Bob	block	pop	cot
rob	smock	drop	trot
jobs	clocks	mops	plots
mobs	locks	stops	dots

Pronunciation Tip

Short *o* is a low back vowel. Drop your jaw when you say short *o*.

Pattern Review 1

To make a noun plural, we usually add - ____.

Listen and Write 1

Listen and fill in the missing letters.

1. clo____	5. ____ob	9. To____
2. do____	6. ____od	10. Ro____
3. sco____	7. ____op	11. ho____
4. do____	8. ____og	12. blo____

Pattern Review 2

At the end of a short-vowel syllable, the sound [k] is spelled - ____, [č] is spelled - ____, [ǰ] is spelled - ____, and [l] is spelled -____.

Add an Ending 1

Change each noun to plural. Write the plural nouns on the lines.

1. bit ____________	3. drop ____________	5. doll ____________
2. block ____________	4. stack ____________	6. cuff ____________

Add an Ending 2

Change these nouns to plural by adding *-es*. Write the plural nouns on the lines. Then complete the Pattern Discovery.

1. dish ____________ 3. lash ____________ 5. kiss ____________
2. match ____________ 4. class ____________ 6. rush ____________

Pattern Discovery 1

If a word ends with -___, -___, or -___, form the plural by adding *-es*. When we form the plural with -___, we add an extra syllable when we say the word.

Listening Discrimination

Pronounce these plural nouns with your teacher. After each word, write the number of syllables on the line.

1. tacks ___	4. stitches ___	7. dots ___	10. hutches ___
2. riches ___	5. bushes ___	8. gashes ___	11. clips ___
3. cliffs ___	6. clocks ___	9. classes ___	12. stops ___

Sight Words

Study the spelling of these numbers. Write each one four times on separate sheet of paper.

seven	eight	nine	ten	eleven	twelve

Add an Ending 3

Change these *-dge* words to plural, and write the plural words on the lines. Notice what happens.

1. bridge ________________ 3. badge ________________
2. ridge ________________ 4. lodge ________________

Pattern Discovery 2

When a one-syllable word ends with *-dge,* add -___ to make it plural. The plural form has ___ syllables.

Listen and Write 2

Write the numbers and plural nouns you hear.

1. ______________ ______________
2. ______________ ______________
3. ______________ ______________
4. ______________ ______________
5. ______________ ______________
6. ______________ ______________

Find the Base Form

Write the singular form of the nouns.

1. tricks ______________
2. bills ______________
3. passes ______________
4. ridges ______________
5. judges ______________
6. rashes ______________
7. pitches ______________
8. lodges ______________

Listen and Write 3

Write the plural nouns you hear. The vowels are short *a* and short *o*.

1. ______________
2. ______________
3. ______________
4. ______________
5. ______________
6. ______________
7. ______________
8. ______________

■ Lesson 8: Short *e*

Words

Pronounce these words with your teacher.

get	bed	end	deck
jet	red	blend	neck
set	shed	spend	speck
ten	beg	best	bent
men	leg	nest	rent
then	peg	test	spent

Pronunciation Tip 1

Short *e* is a mid front vowel. Compare it with short *i* (high front) and short *a* (low front) in these sets of words:

pit — pet — pat   lid — led — lad   him — hem — ham

Pronunciation Tip 2

Combinations like *bl-* and *sp-* at the beginning of a word and *-st*, *-nd*, and *-nt* at the end of a word are called **consonant blends**. Don't insert a vowel sound between the two consonants in a blend.

Pattern Review 1

Short-vowel words have ___ vowel per syllable.

Visual Discrimination

Notice the ends of these one-syllable words. Circle each word that ends with just one consonant.

1. net	5. wreck	9. men
2. best	6. peg	10. peck
3. fed	7. sent	11. flesh
4. when	8. tend	12. fret

Pattern Discovery

The circled words belong to a special category of words known as one-one-one words, or 1-1-1 words. 1-1-1 words have ___ syllable, ___ vowel, and ___ consonant at the end. Notice that we cannot hear whether a word is a 1-1-1 word; we must look at the word and count the letters.

Sight Words

Study the spelling of these ordinal numbers.

first	second	third	fourth	fifth

Listening Discrimination

Pronounce these short *e* words with your teacher. After each word, write the number of syllables on the line. The words have one or two syllables.

1. crest ____
2. better ____
3. sledding ____
4. jets ____
5. fleck ____
6. nesting ____
7. pens ____
8. mended ____
9. get ____

Sight Words

Fill the blanks using ordinal numbers.

1. The word *spent* has five letters. The ____________ letter is *t*.
   The ____________ letter is *p*. The ____________ letter is *s*.
2. The word *wreck* has five letters. The ____________ letter, *w*, is silent.
   The ____________ letter is *e*. The ____________ letter is *k*.
3. The word *mend* has four letters. The ____________ letter is *d*.
   The ____________ letter is *n*. The ____________ letter is *m*.
   The ____________ letter is *e*.

Listen and Write 1

Listen and fill in the missing consonants.

1. ____et	4. pe____	7. ____ed
2. ____en	5. tre____	8. ____end
3. ____eck	6. wre____	9. ____est

Pattern Review 2

Pronounce these words with your teacher, and then look at them carefully. Circle the words that fit the 1-1-1 (one-one-one) pattern. Remember, 1-1-1 words have ____ syllable, ____ vowel, and ____ consonant at the end.

1. betting	4. blender	7. leg
2. pen	5. crested	8. tent
3. sled	6. speck	9. jet

Listen and Write 2

Write the short *e* words you hear.

1. ____________	4. ____________	7. ____________
2. ____________	5. ____________	8. ____________
3. ____________	6. ____________	9. ____________

Listen and Write 3

Listen and fill in the short *e* words and ordinal numbers from this lesson.

I put five short *e* words in alphabetical order. The ___________word is___________. The ___________word is ___________. The ___________word is ___________. The ___________word is ___________. And the ___________word is ___________.

■ Lesson 9: Short *a*, Short *o*, and Short *e* in Contrast

Words

Pronounce these words with your teacher.

pat	lag	knack	badge	hatch	pass	
pot	log	knock	dodge	scotch		doll
pet	leg	neck	hedge	sketch	mess	smell

Pattern Review 1

At the end of a short-vowel syllable, [k] is spelled - ____, [ǰ] is spelled -____, [č] is spelled - ____, [s] is spelled - ____, and [l] is spelled -____.

Add an Ending 1

Change each noun to plural. Write the plural nouns on the lines. Complete the Pattern Review.

1. net ____________
2. clock ____________
3. bell ____________
4. badge ____________
5. doll ____________
6. lodge ____________
7. tag ____________
8. shell ____________
9. hedge ____________

Pattern Review 2

To make a noun plural, we usually add -____. When we add -*s* to -*dge* words, we add an extra ________________ when we say the word.

Add an Ending 2

Change each noun to plural. Write the plural nouns on the lines. Complete the Pattern Review.

1. class ____________
2. sketch ____________
3. mess ____________
4. dash ____________
5. hatch ____________
6. blotch ____________
7. glass ____________
8. dress ____________
9. patch ____________

Pattern Review 3

If a word ends with -____, -____, or -____, form the plural by adding *-es*. We add an extra __________________ when we say the word.

Sight Words

Study the spelling of these numbers, and use them to complete the sentences.

thirteen	fourteen	fifteen	sixteen

Which birthday is best? Some people think turning __________________ (13) is important because that is the first of the "teen" years. People in some Latin American countries have a special celebration when a girl turns __________________(15), while in the United States it's common to have a sweet __________________ (16) celebration. What is special about turning __________________ (14)?

Listening Discrimination

Circle the words or names you hear.

1. sat	set	sod	4. nets	knocks	knacks
2. Ben	bomb	ban	5. messes	masses	meshes
3. etches	edges	hedges	6. bends	bands	bonds

Listen and Write 1

Listen and fill in the missing letters. All of the words are plural.

1. sme________
2. we________
3. blo________
4. ba________
5. ________esses
6. ________ocks
7. ________atches
8. ________obs
9. pa________
10. sta________
11. fle________
12. cre________

Listen and Write 2

Write the numbers and plural nouns you hear.

1. ________________ ________________
2. ________________ ________________
3. ________________ ________________
4. ________________ ________________
5. ________________ ________________
6. ________________ ________________

Pattern Review 4

Pronounce these words and names with your teacher, and then look at them carefully. Circle the words that fit the 1-1-1 pattern. Remember, 1-1-1 words have ___ syllable, ___ vowel, and ___ consonant at the end.

1. deck	5. fender	9. yellow	13. pencil
2. splat	6. clod	10. Tom	14. drop
3. job	7. blog	11. Bob	15. past
4. staff	8. wedge	12. Tess	16. swept

Find the Base Form

Write the singular form of the nouns on the lines.

1. patches ____________	5. lodges ____________
2. hedges ____________	6. classes ____________
3. crashes ____________	7. badges ____________
4. sketches ____________	8. bells ____________

■ Lesson 10: *R*-Controlled Short Vowels

Words

Pronounce these words with your teacher.

clerk	burn	bird	word	for	car
germ	curl	first	work	born	far
her	fur	sir	world	cork	sharp
term	surf	dirt	worth	storm	arch

Pattern Discovery 1

The five short vowels have different sounds when they are followed, or "controlled," by the letter ___.

Pattern Discovery 2

The combinations *-er, -ur,* and *-ir* (as in *clerk, burn,* and *bird*) have the same sound / different sounds (circle one).

Pattern Discovery 3

The combination *-or* after the letter *w* (as in *work*) sounds the same as/ different from (circle one) *-er, -ur,* and *-ir* (as in *clerk, burn,* and *bird*).

Pattern Discovery 4

The combination *-or* makes the same sound / a different sound (circle one) depending on whether it follows the letter *w* or another letter.

Pattern Discovery 5

The combination *-ar* makes the same sound as / a different sound from (circle one) *-er, -ur,* and *-ir*.

Pattern Discovery 6

R-controlled short vowels make ___ different sounds. They are represented phonetically as [ər], [or], and [ar].

Listening Discrimination 1

Circle the words or names you hear.

1. four	fourteen	forty	4. perch	burst	birth
2. her	hurt	Hurst	5. car	card	cart
3. first	fern	fur	6. curl	church	churn

Pronunciation Tip

The sound made by *-er, -ur,* and *-ir* is closest to short *u*. Compare the sounds in these sets of words.

burn — bun	shirt — shut	stern — stun	lurk — luck	clerk — cluck

Pattern Discovery 7

When the sounds [k] or [č] follow a short vowel, we write -____ and -____. However, when the sounds [k] or [č] follow a consonant like *r* or *n,* we write *-k* or *-ch.*

Listening Discrimination 2

Circle the words or names you hear.

1. her	hurt	hut	4. burn	burst	bust
2. fern	fun	first	5. cluck	clerk	Kirk
3. stern	stun	squirt	6. bud	bird	Burt

Sight Words

Study the spelling of these numbers, and use them to complete the sentences.

twenty	thirty	forty	fifty	sixty

1. The fee is ____________ dollars (20) per term.
2. More than ____________ (40) clerks work there.
3. There were ____________ (60) girls in my school.
4. I counted ____________ (50) cars in the parking lot.
5. We sat on the porch for about ____________ (30) minutes.

Choose and Write

Use the words in the box to complete the sentences.

barks	church	perch	world
bird	first	storm	worse
cars	Hurst	work	yard

1. When my dog is in the ____________, he ____________ at ____________ that drive by.
2. Ms. ____________ travels around the ____________ for her____________.
3. The ____________ sat on the ____________ in the cage.
4. I remember the ____________ ____________ that I visited.
5. The____________ was ____________than expected.

Listen and Write

Write the *r*-controlled short-vowel words you hear.

1. ____________
2. ____________
3. ____________
4. ____________
5. ____________
6. ____________
7. ____________
8. ____________
9. ____________

Pattern Review

Circle the words that fit the 1-1-1 pattern.

1. stern
2. bar
3. stir
4. work
5. corn
6. star
7. turn
8. scar
9. perk

■ Unit 2 Review Pages

PATTERN RECAP

1. Short-vowel words have____ vowel per syllable.
   - Pattern exception: Words ending with the [ǰ] sound end with *-dge*.
2. At the end of a short-vowel syllable, we write -____ to spell the sound [k].
   - Pattern exception: When a consonant like *l, n, r,* or *s* appears before the [k] sound, we write -____.
3. At the end of a short-vowel syllable, we write -____ to spell the sound [ǰ].
4. At the end of a short-vowel syllable, we usually write -____ to spell the sound [č].
   - Pattern exception: When a consonant like *r* or *n* appears before the [č] sound, we write -____.
5. We write -____ to spell the sound [š].
6. At the end of a short-vowel word, we write -____ to spell the sound [f].
7. At the end of a short-vowel word, we write -____ to spell the sound [l].
8. At the end of a short-vowel word, we usually write -____ to spell the sound [s].
9. We usually add -____ to make a noun plural. However, if a word ends with -____, -____, or -____, we add *-es* to make the word plural.
10. When we make *-dge* words plural or add *-es* for plural, we add an extra ________________ when we say the word.
11. A special category of words is known as 1-1-1 (one-one-one) words. These words have one ________________, one ________________ in the middle, and end with one ________________.
12. If the letter ____ appears after a short vowel, it changes the sound of the vowel. These vowels are known as *r*-controlled vowels.
13. The sound [ər] can be spelled -____, -____, -____, and sometimes *-or*, after the letter *w*.
14. The sound [or] is usually spelled -____.
15. We write -____ to spell the sound [ar].

Find the Base Form

Write the singular form of each noun on the line.

1. rashes ____________
2. tracks ____________
3. batches ____________
4. passes ____________
5. pets ____________
6. dolls ____________
7. arches ____________
8. docks ____________
9. badges ____________
10. clerks ____________
11. hedges ____________
12. porches ____________
13. decks ____________
14. hatches ____________
15. storms ____________
16. lodges ____________
17. sketches ____________
18. staffs ____________

Vowel Review

Pronounce these sets of words with your teacher. Identify each vowel sound. Listen for the order of sounds in consonant blends.

1. bin	Ben	ban	bun	Bond
2. strip	strep	strap	strum	storm
3. skid	sketch	skirt	skunk	scan
4. limp	lamp	lump	lark	lurk
5. blank	blink	blend	blond	blurt
6. brink	brick	brim	burn	bun
7. stiff	shelf	staff	surf	stuff
8. bridge	hedge	badge	fudge	lodge

Listen and Write

Write the words or names you hear. The words are used in the previous exercise.

1. ____________
2. ____________
3. ____________
4. ____________
5. ____________
6. ____________
7. ____________
8. ____________
9. ____________
10. ____________
11. ____________
12. ____________

Pattern Review

Circle the words that fit the 1-1-1 pattern.

1. match
2. term
3. class
4. fur
5. pack
6. splash
7. knob
8. dirt
9. word
10. tar
11. plot
12. jet
13. shed
14. blend
15. pat
16. log
17. dodge
18. sketch
19. pass
20. doll
21. drop

Listening Discrimination

Pronounce these short-vowel words with your teacher. After each word, write the number of syllables on the line. The words have one or two syllables.

1. matches ____
2. track ____
3. clocks ____
4. splash ____
5. classes ____
6. robbing ____
7. dropper ____
8. best ____
9. ending ____
10. renter ____
11. spent ____
12. Thursday ____
13. forty ____
14. hedge ____
15. pots ____
16. badges ____
17. sketches ____
18. smells ____
19. worth ____
20. thirty ____
21. ending ____

Sight Word Review

Write out the numbers in the boxes next to the numerals.

7		3rd		16	
8		4th		20	
11		5th		30	
12		13		40	
1st		14		50	
2nd		15		60	

Add an Ending

Change each noun to plural. Write the plural nouns on the lines.

1. splash ____________
2. crack ____________
3. scratch ____________
4. pass ____________
5. knob ____________
6. block ____________
7. plot ____________
8. bed ____________
9. nest ____________
10. speck ____________
11. log ____________
12. test ____________
13. dodge ____________
14. latch ____________
15. hedge ____________
16. sketch ____________
17. mess ____________
18. germ ____________
19. curl ____________
20. bird ____________
21. world ____________
22. cork ____________
23. arch ____________
24. smell ____________

Word Builder Puzzle

Create words by selecting a consonant blend or digraph from the left column, a vowel from the middle column, and a consonant or consonant blend from the right column. How many words can you create? Many combinations are possible words. Check to see that you have made real words by asking your teacher, looking in a dictionary, or using a computer's spell-check feature.

sc		ck
sh	i	d
shr	e	ff
sk	a	ft
sl	u	g
sn	o	m
sp	ir	mp
squ	ar	n
st	or	nk
sw		p
		tch

Unit 3

Consonant Doubling

■ Unit 3 Overview

SHORT-VOWEL REVIEW

Benjamin Franklin, who is considered one of the founders of the United States of America, published many short, inspirational sayings. Read these four with your teacher. Notice the words in **bold.**

- ❑ Beware of little expenses. A small leak will **sink** a great **ship.**
- ❑ The **things** which **hurt, instruct.**
- ❑ You will find the key to **success** under the alarm **clock.**
- ❑ We are all **born** ignorant, but we **must** work **hard** to remain stupid.

Discuss the short-vowel words from the sayings. Identify the vowels, and count the syllables. Find one 1-1-1 word.

Example: *little* = short *i*, two syllables

1. sink
2. ship
3. things
4. hurt
5. instruct
6. success
7. clock
8. born
9. must
10. hard

Pattern Review

Short-vowel words have ____ vowel per syllable.

Now read this short description about Benjamin Franklin, and notice the words in bold.

> In the 18th century, Benjamin Franklin was **living** and **working** in Philadelphia. He **worked** in many fields. He **published** his sayings in a newspaper. He is also famous for **experimenting** with electricity and **inventing** the lightning rod. He also **started** the first fire department in Pennsylvania.

Pattern Discovery

The bold words in the reading have two endings: -____ and -____. The -____ ending shows that a verb is past tense. It is also used to create adjectives. The -____ ending shows that a verb is in progressive form. It is also used to form gerunds and to create adjectives.

Application

Discuss sayings that you know or that you translate from your language. Can you find short-vowel words in the sayings?

■ Lesson 11: Adding *-s, -ed,* and *-ing*

Words

Pronounce these words with your teacher. They are all verbs.

hit	tuck	catch	stop	help	stir	star
pick	rub	splash	spot	sell	turn	start
dip	buff	plan	rock	press	blur	scar

Pattern Review 1

Short-vowel words have ____ vowel per syllable.

Add an Ending 1

Add *-s* or *-es* to these verbs to change them to third person singular form. Write the verbs on the lines. Complete the Pattern Expansion.

1. hit ____________
2. pick ____________
3. buff ____________
4. catch ____________
5. splash ____________
6. stop ____________
7. sell ____________
8. stir ____________
9. press ____________

Pattern Expansion

We add -____ or -____ to make a noun plural. We also add -____ or -____ to change a verb to third person singular. Follow the same rule: We usually add -____. However, if a word ends with -____, -____, or -____, we add *-es,* and we add an extra syllable when we pronounce the word.

Add an Ending 2

Add *-ed* to these verbs. Write the verbs on the lines.

1. pick ____________
2. buff ____________
3. splash ____________
4. turn ____________
5. help ____________
6. press ____________

Pronunciation Tip

When you add *-ed,* do not add an extra syllable when you say the word, unless *-ed* comes after *-t* or *-d.*

Add an Ending 3

Add *-ing* to these verbs. Write the verbs on the lines.

1. stick ____________
2. stuff ____________
3. crash ____________
4. turn ____________
5. help ____________
6. stress ____________

Pattern Review 2

A special category of words is known as 1-1-1 (one-one-one) words. These words have one ______________, one ______________ in the middle, and end with one ______________. Write the 1-1-1 words from the list at the beginning of the lesson (page 45) on these lines:

____________ ____________

____________ ____________

____________ ____________

____________ ____________

____________ ____________

Pattern Discovery 1

Study what happens when we add *-ed* or *-ing* to a 1-1-1 word, and complete the pattern.

dip → dipped rub → rubbed stop → stopped

hit → hitting plan → planning stir → stirring

When we add *-ed* or *-ing* to a 1-1-1 word, we double the final ______________.

Add an Ending 4

Double the final consonant, and write the indicated ending to these 1-1-1 words.

1. sit + ing ____________
2. zip + ed ____________
3. trim + ing ____________
4. kid + ing ____________
5. hug + ed ____________
6. stun + ed ____________
7. cut + ing ____________
8. clap + ing ____________
9. rob + ed ____________
10. drop + ed ____________
11. beg + ing ____________
12. get + ing ____________
13. star + ing ____________
14. stir + ed ____________

Sight Words

Study the spelling of these months, and use them to complete the sentences.

January	February	March	April

1. ________________ is the second month. It comes after ________________.
2. ________________ is the fourth month. It comes after ________________.
3. The third month is ________________. It comes after ________________.
4. The first month is ________________. It comes before ________________.

Pattern Discovery 2

Names of months begin with capital / small (circle one) letters.

Find the Base Form

Take off the endings, and write the base form of the verbs on the lines.

1. catches ____________
2. hitting ____________
3. starred ____________
4. plans ____________
5. trucking ____________
6. blurred ____________
7. trucking ____________
8. starts ____________
9. helping ____________
10. buffed ____________
11. passed ____________
12. splashes ____________
13. smelled ____________
14. stirring ____________
15. presses ____________
16. rocked ____________

■ Lesson 12: Adding Other Endings with Vowels

Words

Pronounce these words with your teacher. Notice the vowels and consonant patterns.

quick	pick	cut	sad	rob
quit	trick	fun	mad	hot
quilt	stick	shut	track	Bob
squish	Rick	sun	fast	Tom

Pattern Discovery 1

The sound [kw] is spelled -____. In this case, the letter *u* is not considered a vowel, so words like *quick* are short-vowel words, and *quit* is a 1-1-1 word.

Listen and Write 1

Listen and fill in the missing letters.

1. sti____	4. ____ick	7. ____int
2. squi____	5. ____ick	8. ____ack
3. fa____	6. ____ut	9. ____at

Add an Ending 1

Add *-er* to these words. Write the words on the lines.

1. stick ______________ 2. quilt ______________ 3. pick ______________

Pattern Discovery 2

Add -____ to a verb to create a noun.

Add an Ending 2

Add *-er* to these words. Write the words on the lines.

1. quick ______________ 2. fast ______________ 3. thick ______________

Pattern Discovery 3

Add -____ to an adjective to change it to the comparative form.

Add an Ending 3

Add *-est* to these words. Write the words on the lines.

1. quick ____________ 2. fast ____________ 3. thick ____________

Pattern Discovery 4

Add - ____ to an adjective to change it to the superlative form.

Pattern Review

Pronounce these words with your teacher. Look at them carefully. Circle the words that fit the 1-1-1 pattern. Remember, 1-1-1 words have ____ syllable, ____ vowel, and ____ consonant at the end.

quick	cut	rob	stick	stack
pick	sad	quilt	truck	hot

Add an Ending 4

Double the final consonant, and write the indicated ending to these 1-1-1 words. Complete the Pattern Revision.

1. hit + er ____________
2. red + est ____________
3. shut + er ____________
4. sun + y ____________
5. sad + est ____________
6. Bob + y ____________
7. quit + er ____________
8. cut + er ____________
9. fun + y ____________
10. mad + est ____________
11. Tom + y ____________
12. rob + er ____________

Pattern Revision

When we add an ending that begins with a vowel *(-ed, -ing, -er, -est, -y)* to a 1-1-1 word, we double the final ________________.

Sight Words

Study the spelling of these months, and use them in the following exercise.

May	June	July	August

Listen and Write 2

Write the names, *-ing* forms, and months you hear.

1. ____________ went ____________ last ______________.
2. ____________ went ____________ last ______________.
3. ____________ went ____________ last ______________.
4. ____________ went ____________ last ______________.

Find the Base Form

Take off the *-y* endings and, write the base form of the words on the lines.

1. sunny ____________
2. windy ____________
3. funny ____________
4. picky ____________
5. Bobby ____________
6. starry ____________
7. rusty ____________
8. choppy ____________
9. Billy ____________
10. fussy ____________
11. smelly ____________
12. patchy ____________

Listen and Write 3

Write the two-syllable short-vowel words you hear, and complete the Pattern Discovery.

1. ____________
2. ____________
3. ____________
4. ____________
5. ____________
6. ____________

Pattern Discovery 5

Short-vowel words with two syllables have ____ consonants, or a double consonant, in the middle. Circle the consonants in the middle of each word you wrote.

■ Lesson 13: -VCC + *-le* Pattern

Words

Pronounce these words with your teacher. Notice the vowels and consonant patterns.

little	puddle	settle	paddle	bottle	gargle
dribble	ruffle	pebble	babble	cobble	marble
middle	struggle	freckle	battle	goggle	hurdle
pickle	buckle	kettle	tackle	topple	burgle

Pronunciation Tip

When *-dd-* and *-tt-* appear in the middle of a word, the pronunciation is very similar: your tongue hits the roof of your mouth briefly when you make this sound.

Pattern Review

Short-vowel words with two syllables have ____ consonants, or a ___________ consonant, in the middle.

Pattern Discovery

Notice the pattern in the words on the list. It is -VCC + *-le*. That is, the words

❑ start with a vowel or one or more consonants
❑ have ____ vowel in the first syllable
❑ are followed by ____ consonants (or a double consonant)
❑ They end with the letters -____.

The sound [əl] is most often represented by -____ at the end of a word.

Listen and Write 1

Listen and fill in the missing consonants.

1. chu____le	4. ra____le	7. ha____le
2. cri____le	5. da____le	8. ju____le
3. fi____le	6. ji____le	9. di____le

Listen and Write 2

Listen and fill in the missing vowel.

1. r__ddle	4. k__ttle	7. l__ttle
2. m__ddle	5. h__ssle	8. str__ggle
3. j__ggle	6. b__bble	9. g__ggle

Sight Words 3

Study the spelling of these months, and use them to complete the sentences.

September	October	November	December

Listen and Write 3

Write the months and -VCC + *-le* words you hear.

1. They held a ____________ last ______________.
2. Fall begins in the ____________ of ______________.
3. They pick ____________ in ______________.
4. The weather in ____________ is a ______________ cool.

Listen and Write 4

Write the -VCC + *le* words you hear.

1. ______________	7. ______________	13. ______________
2. ______________	8. ______________	14. ______________
3. ______________	9. ______________	15. ______________
4. ______________	10. ______________	16. ______________
5. ______________	11. ______________	17. ______________
6. ______________	12. ______________	18. ______________

Choose and Write

Use -VCC + *-le* words to complete the lines from nursery rhymes. Some words are used more than once. If you can't guess, ask your teacher or look up the rhymes on the Internet.

buckle	dumpling	little	turtle
bumblebee	fiddle	nimble	twinkle twinkle
candlestick	Jingleheimer	puddles	
diddle diddle	kettle	tumbling	

1. ____________ Jack Horner sat in a corner; eating his mincemeat pie.
2. Hey, ____________ ____________ the cat and the____________.
3. ____________ dee dee, ____________ dee dee; the fly has married the ____________.
4. One, two ____________ my shoe; three, four knock at the door.
5. ____________ ____________ ______________ my son John, went to bed with his trousers on.
6. Polly put the ____________ on; we'll all have tea.
7. Jack be ____________, Jack be quick; Jack jump over the ______________.
8. John Jacob ______________ Schmidt; his name is my name, too!
9. ____________, ____________ ____________ star; how I wonder what you are.
10. There was a ____________ ____________ who lived in a box. He swam in the ______________ and climbed on the rocks.
11. Jack fell down and broke his crown, and Jill came ______________ after.

Sight Word Review

Write the names of the months of the year in order.

1. ______________	5. ______________	9. ______________
2. ______________	6. ______________	10. ______________
3. ______________	7. ______________	11. ______________
4. ______________	8. ______________	12. ______________

■ Lesson 14: *E*-Drop

Words

Pronounce these words with your teacher. Notice the endings.

lodge	dodge	edge	settle	wrinkle
lodged	dodged	edged	settler	wrinkled
lodger	dodger	edging	settled	wrinkling
lodging	dodging	edgy	settling	wrinkly

Pattern Discovery

When a word ends with *e,* we drop the ____ before adding an ending that begins with a vowel, such as *-ed, -er, -ing,* and *-y.*

Find the Base Form 1

Take off the endings, and write the base form of the words on the lines.

1. judges ____________	5. hedges ____________	9. wobbly ____________
2. fudging ____________	6. budging ____________	10. toddler ____________
3. juggling ____________	7. drizzling ____________	11. kettles ____________
4. lodging ____________	8. buckled ____________	12. hedging ____________

Pattern Review 1

Circle the 1-1-1 words, and underline the words that end with *-e.*

1. back	4. bumble	7. edge	10. tickle
2. pet	5. log	8. cut	11. bottle
3. badge	6. stick	9. pat	12. hit

Find the Base Form 2

Take off the endings, and write the base form of the words on the lines.

1. backed ____________
2. petting ____________
3. badges ____________
4. bumbling ____________
5. logger ____________
6. sticky ____________
7. edgy ____________
8. cutter ____________
9. patting ____________
10. ticklish ____________
11. bottling ____________
12. hitter ____________

Pattern Expansion

- When adding an ending beginning with a vowel (*-ed, -ing, -er, -est, -ish,* or *-y*) to a 1-1-1 word, ____________ the final consonant.
- When adding an ending beginning with a vowel to a word that ends with the letter -____, drop the ____.

Sight Words

Fill in the names of the months and study the abbreviations.

________________ = Jan. ________________ = Mar.

________________ = Feb. ________________ = Apr.

Listen and Write 1

Write the one-syllable short-vowel words you hear. Circle the 1-1-1 words.

1. ____________
2. ____________
3. ____________
4. ____________
5. ____________
6. ____________
7. ____________
8. ____________
9. ____________
10. ____________
11. ____________
12. ____________
13. ____________
14. ____________
15. ____________
16. ____________
17. ____________
18. ____________
19. ____________
20. ____________
21. ____________

Add an Ending

Pay special attention to consonant doubling and *e*-drop. Add the indicated ending to these one- and two-syllable short-vowel words.

1. wit + y ________________
2. grin + ed ________________
3. red + ish ________________
4. scrub + er ________________
5. fun + y ________________
6. judge + ing ________________
7. gum + y ________________
8. spin + ing ________________
9. lodge + er ________________
10. splash + ing ________________
11. chop + er ________________
12. flat + est ________________
13. stiff + er ________________
14. girl + ish ________________
15. stop + ed ________________
16. clutch + ed ________________
17. fiddle + er ________________
18. bottle + ing ________________
19. battle + ed ________________
20. tickle + ish ________________

Listen and Write 2

Write the two-syllable short-vowel words you hear, and then complete the Pattern Review.

1. ________________
2. ________________
3. ________________
4. ________________
5. ________________
6. ________________
7. ________________
8. ________________
9. ________________

Pattern Review 2

In a two-syllable word, a short vowel in the first syllable is almost always followed by ____ consonants (like *-ck, -rk,* or *-st*), or by a ________________ consonant (like *-pp* or *-dd*).

This is one of the most powerful spelling rules in English!

❑ Remember: Short vowel + 2 consonants! Remember: -VCCV-

■ Lesson 15: Adding Endings with Consonants

Words

Pronounce these words with your teacher. Notice the endings.

quick	quickly	sad	sadness	harm	harmless
sick	sickly	red	redness	top	topless
warm	warmly	glad	gladness	guilt	guiltless
firm	firmly	stiff	stiffness	rest	restless
glum	glumly	ill	illness	sin	sinless
sharp	sharply	well	wellness	help	helpless

Pattern Discovery 1

Add - ____ to an adjective to change it to an adverb.

Pattern Discovery 2

Add - ____ to an adjective to change it to a noun.

Pattern Discovery 3

Add - ____ to a noun to change it to an adjective (meaning "without").

Pattern Discovery 4

When we add an ending beginning with a ________________, we do not double the final consonant.

Pattern Expansion 1

-VCCV- is a very common pattern in short-vowel words, as we saw in the previous lessons. Some examples of this pattern from the list are *gladness*, ________________, and ________________ . It is also possible to have a -VCCCV- pattern, when we add an ending that begins with a consonant to a word that ends with ____ consonants, such as *-ck* or *-ff*.

Add an Ending 1

Write the words using the indicated endings.

1. glad + ly __________	7. ill + ness __________
2. glad + ness __________	8. rest + less __________
3. firm + ly __________	9. restless + ness __________
4. firm + ness __________	10. effort + less __________
5. thick + ly __________	11. effortless + ness __________
6. thick + ness __________	12. effortless + ly __________

Pattern Expansion 2

The ending -*ness* and the ending -*ly* may be added after the ending - ____. This makes it easy to spell some very long words! Notice:

help + less + ness = helplessness	help + less + ly = helplessly
harm + less + ness = __________	harm + less + ly = __________

Sight Words

Fill in the names of the months, and study the abbreviations.

__________ = Aug.	__________ = Nov.
__________ = Sept.	__________ = Dec.
__________ = Oct.	

Find the Base Form

Take off the endings, and write the base form of the words on the lines.

1. gruffness __________	9. reddish __________
2. stiffly __________	10. redness __________
3. cuffs __________	11. reddest __________
4. stuffing __________	12. redder __________
5. ticker __________	13. saddest __________
6. thickness __________	14. sadly __________
7. backless __________	15. sadness __________
8. wrecker __________	16. sadder __________

Listen and Write

Write the words you hear. Note whether the word is a base form or has an ending.

1. ________ 7. ________ 13. ________
2. ________ 8. ________ 14. ________
3. ________ 9. ________ 15. ________
4. ________ 10. ________ 16. ________
5. ________ 11. ________ 17. ________
6. ________ 12. ________ 18. ________

Add an Ending 2

Write the words using the indicated endings. Pay special attention to consonant doubling.

1. map + ing ________
2. thin + er ________
3. sun + less ________
4. slug + ish ________
5. red + ness ________
6. club + ed ________
7. fat + est ________
8. firm + ly ________

Add Two Endings

Write the words using the two indicated endings. Pay special attention to consonant doubling.

1. red + ish + ness ________
2. stun + ing + ly ________
3. job + less + ness ________
4. fit + ing + ly ________
5. help + less + ly ________
6. end + less + ness ________

■ Unit 3 Review Pages

PATTERN RECAP

1. Endings change the forms of words.
   -____ can show that a verb is past tense.
   -____ can show that a verb is in progressive form, or that it is a gerund.
   -____ or -____ can make a noun plural or make a verb agree with third person singular.
   -____ changes a verb to a noun.
   -____ changes an adjective to comparative form.
   -____ changes an adjective to superlative form.
   -*y* changes a ______________ into an adjective.
   -*ish* creates an ________________.
   -*ly* changes an ________________ to an adverb.
   -____ changes an adjective to a noun.
   -____ changes a noun to an adjective (with the meaning *without*).
2. 1-1-1 words have ____ syllable, ____ vowel, and end with ____ consonant.
3. When we add an ending that begins with a ________________ to a 1-1-1 word, we ______________ the final consonant. When we add an ending that begins with a consonant, we do ____ double the final consonant.
4. When we add an ending that begins with a vowel to a word than ends with the letter -*e*, we drop the -____ before adding the ending.
5. The sound [əl] at the end of a two-syllable short-vowel word is usually spelled -____.
6. In a two-syllable word, a short vowel in the first syllable is almost always followed by ____ consonants or by a double ________________.

Ending Review

Circle the ending on each word. Tell the function of the ending and if any changes were made to the base word when the ending was added.

1. sickness	7. churches	13. sunny
2. ticklish	8. scratches	14. quickly
3. hottest	9. planted	15. wobbly
4. edger	10. stopped	16. curtly
5. sharper	11. giggling	17. sunless
6. words	12. itches	18. stormy

Sight Word Review

Write the name of the month next to the abbreviation.

Jan. ________________	Sept. ________________
Feb. ________________	Oct. ________________
Mar. ________________	Nov. ________________
Apr. ________________	Dec. ________________
Aug. ________________	

Which months do not have abbreviations (because the names are already short)?

________________ ________________ ________________

Add an Ending/Find the Base Form

In the middle column, write the word with the indicated ending. Then cover the left column, and write the base form in the right column. Uncover to check your work.

1. hit + er __________ __________
2. pick + s or + es __________ __________
3. buff + er __________ __________
4. plan + ing __________ __________
5. spot + less __________ __________
6. blur + y __________ __________
7. star + ing __________ __________
8. harm + less __________ __________
9. rub + ed __________ __________
10. zip + er __________ __________
11. catch + s or + es __________ __________
12. quick + ly __________ __________
13. quit + er __________ __________
14. squish + y __________ __________
15. sun + y __________ __________
16. hill + y __________ __________
17. rich + ness __________ __________
18. pickle + s or + es __________ __________
19. settle + er __________ __________
20. gargle + ing __________ __________
21. tickle + ish __________ __________
22. bottle + ed __________ __________
23. crisp + ness __________ __________
24. hedge + ed __________ __________
25. girl + ish __________ __________

Word Builder Puzzle

Create words by selecting a consonant or consonant blend from the left column, a vowel from the second column, a double consonant or consonant blend/digraph from the third column, and *-le* from the last column. How many words can you create? Any combination that you can make is a possible word. Check to see that you have made real words by asking your teacher, looking in a dictionary, or using a computer's spell-check feature.

		bb	
b, br,		ck	
cr,	i	dd	
d, dr,	u	ff	
f, fr,	a	gg	
g, h,	o	mb	
j, k,	e	mp	le
l, m,		ng	
n, p,		nk	
r, s,		pp	
scr		st	
		tt	

Word Search Puzzle

There are 22 two-syllable short-vowel words in this puzzle. They all appear horizontally; look from left to right. Circle the words, write them at the bottom of the page, and tell at least one fact that you know about each word. One has been done for you as an example.

s	c	a	t	c	h	e	s	r	h	i	n	t	e	d
s	t	i	c	k	y	e	r	s	h	u	t	t	e	r
p	o	p	i	n	s	t	r	u	c	t	l	e	s	s
s	k	o	n	y	e	r	p	l	a	n	n	i	n	g
h	e	l	p	i	n	g	y	l	k	i	d	d	e	d
o	s	u	c	c	e	s	s	r	e	n	s	a	r	t
h	u	l	e	q	u	i	t	t	e	r	e	s	s	e
s	a	d	d	e	s	t	r	f	u	s	s	y	e	r
c	k	e	t	t	l	e	o	p	r	e	s	s	e	s
c	r	a	t	t	r	u	f	f	l	e	a	r	t	s
j	u	g	g	l	i	n	g	t	o	p	l	e	s	s
s	c	r	i	m	p	t	d	u	m	p	l	i	n	g
o	o	l	d	o	d	g	e	r	c	a	n	p	s	e
h	e	l	p	l	e	s	s	o	f	i	r	m	l	y
o	l	i	l	l	n	e	s	s	e	r	n	e	s	s

Example: catches

Catches has a short *a*. Because of the short *a*, it ends with *-tch*. We add *-es* because it ends with *-tch*.

1. ______________
2. ______________
3. ______________
4. ______________
5. ______________
6. ______________
7. ______________
8. ______________
9. ______________
10. ______________
11. ______________
12. ______________
13. ______________
14. ______________
15. ______________
16. ______________
17. ______________
18. ______________
19. ______________
20. ______________
21. ______________
22. ______________

Unit 4

Long-Vowel Silent *e* Pattern

Unit 4 Overview

INTRODUCTION TO LONG VOWELS

Match the following statements about these popular fairy tales, and then discuss the pronunciation and spelling of the words and names in **bold** with your teacher. (Answers are on the bottom of page 66.)

1. Cinderella ____	a. met seven dwarfs.
2. **Sleeping** Beauty ____	b. lived with a **beast**.
3. **Snow White** ____	c. the **true** princess.
4. A beauty **named** Belle ____	d. lost a **shoe**.
5. The Snow **Queen** ____	e. lived **near** the North **Pole**.
6. A **pea** identified ____	f. fell into a **deep** sleep.

Study these words and names, and say the vowel sound in each.

named	deep	White	Pole	true

Pattern Discovery

These one-syllable words have one / two (circle one) vowels.

Say the names of the letters aloud. Circle the vowels. Listen to the names of the letters.

a	b	c	d	e	f	g	h	i	j	k	l	m	n	o	p	q	r	s	t	u	v	w	x	y	z

Pattern Discovery

There are five long vowels in English. One-syllable long-vowel words usually contain ____ vowels. Long vowels sound like the name of the __________. In order to learn to spell long-vowel words, you have to listen for the sound and look for the pattern.

Visual Discrimination

Circle the two vowels in each of these long-vowel words. Which letter does each vowel sound like?

1. sleep
2. snow*
3. white
4. named
5. queen
6. pea
7. beast
8. true
9. shoe
10. pole
11. deep
12. near

*Note that *w* and *y* work like vowels in long-vowel words.

Application

Discuss or write about one of the stories mentioned or one that you know. Look for long vowels in your description.

Answers: 1. d ("Cinderella"); 2. f ("Sleeping Beauty"); 3. a ("Snow White and the Seven Dwarfs"); 4. b ("Beauty and the Beast"); 5. e ("The Snow Queen"); 6. c ("The Princess and the Pea")

■ Lesson 16: Long *a* with Silent e

Words

Pronounce these short *a* words and names with your teacher.

mad Sam back can cap far fat

Now notice what happens when we add a silent *-e* to the end of each word.

made same bake cane cape fare fate

Pattern Discovery 1

A common long *a* pattern is *-aCe,* where the letter *a* is followed by one ________________ and a silent ____.

Pattern Discovery 2

The sound [k] is spelled -____ after a long vowel, but it is spelled -____ at the end of a short-vowel syllable.

Listening Discrimination

Circle the words you hear.

1. tap	tape	4. rack	rake	7. mad	made
2. plan	plane	5. van	vane	8. shack	shake
3. fat	fate	6. hat	hate	9. staff	safe

Pattern Review 1

1-1-1 words have one ________________, one ________________ in the middle, and end with one ________________. Long-vowel words are never 1-1-1 words because they have ____ vowels.

Visual Discrimination

Circle the 1-1-1 words.

1. grade	4. make	7. scam
2. staff	5. stab	8. flat
3. cap	6. slate	9. quack

Listen and Write

Listen and fill in the silent *e* if you hear a long *a* word.

1. grad__	4. cam__	7. shad__
2. scrap__	5. slat__	8. cap__
3. pan__	6. dam__	9. sham__

Sight Words

Study the spelling of these major American cities (and the spelling of your city or town), and use them to complete the sentences.

New York	Chicago	Los Angeles	Miami	________________ (your city)

1. ________________ is in the West.
2. ________________ is in the Northeast.
3. ________________ is in the Midwest region.
4. ________________ is in the Southeast.
5. ________________ is in the ________________ (region).

Pattern Discovery 3

Names of cities begin with capital / small (circle one) letters. If the city name is two words, then the first word is / both words are (circle one) capitalized.

Choose the Best Completion

Read each sentence, and circle the word that best completes it. Say the words aloud, and listen for the vowel sound.

1. When you feel angry you can say that you are mad / made.
2. If you are making cookies you have to back / bake them.
3. A little bit of food that you eat between meals is a snack / snake.
4. You usually wear a cap / cape around your shoulders.
5. One square of glass in a window is a pan / pane.
6. A dam / dame holds water back on a river.
7. An animal that is a little larger than a mouse is a rat / rate.
8. If you scrap / scrape your knee, you should clean it right away.
9. When we went to New York, we took a plan / plane instead of driving.
10. Which stat / state is Chicago in?

Add an Ending 1

Change each noun to plural. Write the plural nouns on the lines.

1. cane ____________	4. fate ____________	7. snake ____________
2. cap ____________	5. staff ____________	8. scrape ____________
3. fare ____________	6. rack ____________	9. slat ____________

Add an Ending 2

Change each verb to third person singular by adding *-s*. Write the verbs on the lines.

1. bake ____________	4. tap ____________	7. hate ____________
2. grade ____________	5. plan ____________	8. snack ____________
3. quake ____________	6. shame ____________	9. make ____________

Pattern Review 2

Add -____ to make a noun ____________ or to make a verb third person singular. Do not drop the silent -____ before adding *-s*.

■ Lesson 17: Long *i* with Silent e

Words

Pronounce these words with your teacher.

bribe	bride	strike	lime	pipe	rise
describe	decide	turnpike	slime	stripe	wise
advice	wife	file	nine	admire	white
nice	knife	while	mine	fire	quite

Pronunciation Tip

The long *i* sound is represented phonetically as [ai]. You may hear [ai], but don't write the letter *a*. Write the letter *i*.

Pattern Discovery

A very common long *i* pattern is *-iCe,* where the letter *i* is followed by one ________________ and a silent ____. This pattern is often found in the second syllable of a two-syllable word.

Listening Discrimination

Circle the words you hear.

1. rid	ride	rod	4. slim	slam	slime
2. like	lock	lick	5. cot	kite	cat
3. Tom	time	tame	6. dine	din	don

Listen and Write 1

Listen and fill in the silent *e* if you hear a long *i* word.

1. fir__	4. slim__	7. dim__
2. rip__	5. rid__	8. win__
3. fin__	6. brib__	9. sit__

Listen and Write 2

Listen and write the two-syllable words with long *i* in the second syllable.

1. ________________ 4. ________________ 7. ________________
2. ________________ 5. ________________ 8. ________________
3. ________________ 6. ________________ 9. ________________

Sight Words

Study the spelling of these state names (and the spelling of your state and a neighboring state), and use them to complete the sentences.

California	Florida	Texas	________________	________________

1. Miami is in ________________, and Los Angeles is in ________________.
2. Houston is in ________________, and I live in ________________.
3. ________________ is next to my state.

Add an Ending 1

Change each noun to plural. Write the plural nouns on the lines.

1. kite ____________ 3. stripe ____________ 5. chime ____________
2. wire ____________ 4. line ____________ 6. bike ____________

Pattern Discovery

Study what happens when we make certain long *i* words plural, and fill in the pattern.

knife → knives wife → wives life → lives

To form the plural of words that end in *-fe* or *-f*, drop the -____ or -____ and add *-ves*.

Add an Ending 2

Change each noun to plural using *-ves*. Write the plural nouns on the lines.

1. knife ____________
2. wife ____________
3. self ____________
4. life ____________
5. shelf ____________
6. scarf ____________
7. elf ____________
8. half ____________
9. calf ____________

Pattern Exception

Not all words ending in -____ or -____ use *-ves* for the plural. Some words just add *-s*. For example,

chief → chiefs cuff → ____________ roof → ____________

Add an Ending 3

Add the long *i* suffix *-ize* to create verbs. Words ending in *-y* drop the *-y* before adding *-ize*. Do not double the final consonant because these are not 1-1-1 words.

1. summary + ize = ________________
2. computer + ize = ________________
3. central + ize = ________________
4. visual + ize = ________________
5. item + ize = ________________
6. harmony + ize = ________________
7. modern + ize = ________________
8. apology + ize = ________________

Find the Base Form

Write the singular forms of the nouns on the lines.

1. sites ____________
2. bribes ____________
3. bibs ____________
4. knives ____________
5. slices ____________
6. stitches ____________
7. scarves ____________
8. wires ____________
9. kits ____________
10. kites ____________
11. wives ____________
12. chiefs ____________
13. tiles ____________
14. hitches ____________
15. lives ____________
16. ticks ____________
17. pills ____________
18. piles ____________

Lesson 18: Long *o* with Silent *e*, Long *o* in Final Syllable

Words

Pronounce these words with your teacher.

globe	joke	home	rope	rose
earlobe	smoke	dome	elope	chose
rode	pole	stone	adore	vote
decode	whole	alone	score	remote

Pronunciation Tip

Long *o* is a rounded vowel. Your lips should form a circle when you say long *o*.

Pattern Discovery 1

A very common long *o* pattern is -*o*C*e*, where the letter *o* is followed by one ________________ and a silent ____.

Pattern Exception

Some words follow the -__C__ pattern but do not have the long *o* sound. Pronounce these words with your teacher.

come	some	one	done	love	lose

Listen and Write 1

Listen and fill in the silent *e* if you hear a long *o* word.

1. rob__	4. ton__	7. cop__
2. cod__	5. hop__	8. rod __
3. tom__	6. not__	9. lob__

Sight Words

Study the spelling of some words you need to write your address.

Street	Avenue	Road	Highway

Listen and Write 2

Listen and fill in the missing names and words.

1. The building is on ____________ ____________ ________________.
2. She lives on ____________ ____________ ____________.
3. The school is on ____________ ________________.
4. She lives on ____________ ____________.
5. It is near West ____________ ________________.

Pattern Discovery 2

Each word in the name of an address begins with a capital letter / a small letter (circle one).

Pattern Discovery 3

Pronounce these words with your teacher. Notice that the last syllable is a long *o*.

1.	2.	3.	4.	5.
stereo	piano	auto	echo	avocado
studio	cello	casino	hero	zero
duo	solo	logo	potato	tornado
trio	soprano	taco	tomato	mango
radio	alto	inferno	torpedo	mosquito
video	banjo	combo	veto	motto

Forming the Plural

When a word of two or more syllables ends with long *o*, there are several options for forming the plural. Study the examples and fill in each Discovery.

Discovery

- *stereos, studios, duos* (List 1)

Words ending in vowel + *o* form the plural by adding -____.

Discovery

- *pianos, cellos, solos* (List 2)

Musical terms ending with -*o* form the plural by adding -____.

Discovery

- *autos, casinos, logos* (List 3)

Many words ending with consonant + *o* form the plural by adding - ____.

Discovery

- *echoes, heroes, potatoes* (List 4)

Some words ending with consonant + *o* form the plural by adding -____.

Discovery

- *avocados/avocadoes, zeros/zeroes, tornados/tornadoes* (List 5)

Some words ending with consonant + *o* form the plural by adding -____ or -____; both plural forms are correct.

Add an Ending

Write the plural form of the long *o* words on the lines. Use the lists and Discoveries to find which pattern the words follow.

1. mosquito ____________________
2. taco ____________________
3. radio ____________________
4. video ____________________
5. alto ____________________
6. auto ____________________
7. tomato ____________________
8. hero ____________________
9. avocado ____________________
10. piano ____________________
11. casino ____________________
12. echo ____________________

Lesson 19: Long *u* with Silent *e*

Words

Pronounce these words with your teacher.

cube	use	introduce	rule
tube	amuse	produce	plume
tune	cute	huge	continue
prune	flute	duke	blue

Pronunciation Tip

Long *u* has two slightly different pronunciations in English. Sometimes it sounds like [u] as in *rule,* and sometimes it sounds like [yu] as in *cute*. Some words have two pronunciations depending on the speaker's dialect. In spite of these differences, both pronunciations are considered long *u*.

Pattern Discovery 1

A common long *u* pattern is -*u*Ce, where the letter *u* is followed by one ________________ and a silent ____. We find this pattern in one-syllable words and as the last syllable in longer words.

Pattern Discovery 2

When long ____ appears at the end of a syllable, the -*ue* pattern is very common.

Listen and Write 1

Listen and fill in the silent *e* if you hear a long *u* word.

1. rud__
2. hug__
3. plum__
4. tun__
5. us__
6. brut__
7. cub__
8. cut__
9. tub__

Listen and Write 2

Listen and write the words with long *u* in the last syllable.

1. ____________________
2. ____________________
3. ____________________
4. ____________________
5. ____________________
6. ____________________
7. ____________________
8. ____________________
9. ____________________

Visual Discrimination

Look at these one-syllable short *u* and long *u* words. Circle the words that fit the 1-1-1 pattern.

1. tub
2. rude
3. huge
4. gull
5. plum
6. dune
7. duck
8. but
9. brute
10. muss
11. muse
12. duke
13. mush
14. much
15. cut
16. cute
17. cuff
18. crust

Sight Words

Practice the spelling of some proper nouns in your life. Write names of places that begin with capital letters. Fill in as many as you can.

Your school: ______________________________

The address of your school: ______________________________

The place where you work: ______________________________

The area you live in (apartment complex, neighborhood): ____________________

Add an Ending

Add *-ing* to the long *u* words. Drop the silent *e*. Write the words on the lines.

1. introduce ________	7. refuse ________
2. amuse ________	8. use ________
3. reduce ________	9. execute ________
4. include ________	10. prune ________
5. rule ________	11. produce ________
6. tune ________	12. reassure ________

Find the Base Form

Take off the endings, and write the base form of the long *u* words on the lines.

1. cutest ________	9. produces ________
2. reusable ________	10. rudest ________
3. insurance ________	11. crudely ________
4. dunes ________	12. ruler ________
5. including ________	13. hugeness ________
6. surely ________	14. useless ________
7. tuner ________	15. excusable ________
8. executed ________	16. tuning ________

Pattern Review and Expansion

- When adding an ending beginning with a ________ to a word that ends with a silent -____, drop the silent - ____. Some endings beginning with vowels in the Find the Base Form exercise include

  -____, -____, -____, -____, -____, -____, -____

- When adding an ending beginning with a ________ to a word that ends with silent -____, keep the silent -____. Some endings beginning with consonants in the Find the Base Form exercise include

  -____, -____,- ____, -____

Pattern Discovery 3

The ending *-ance* makes a word a ________. The ending *-able* makes a word an ________.

Lesson 20: VC*e* for Long *a*, Long *i*, Long *o*, and Long *u*

Words

Pronounce these words with your teacher.

made	wife	globe	cube
safe	nice	code	rude
take	glide	spoke	huge
plane	while	stole	rule
same	mine	hope	dune
slate	stripe	rose	use

Pattern Review 1

The VC*e* pattern is common for long -____, long -____, long -____, and long -____.

Pattern Exception

The VC*e* pattern is not very common for long -____, but we do have a few words that follow the pattern, including *these*, *complete*, and *theme*, and names like *Pete* and *Steve*.

Listen and Write

Listen and fill in the missing vowels.

1. ch__se	4. al__ne	7. br__te	10. w__ne
2. r__le	5. qu__ke	8. str__ke	11. r__te
3. f__ne	6. sw__pe	9. am__se	12. cr__de

Visual Discrimination

Circle the words that fit the 1-1-1 pattern.

rob	plume	slime	can
robe	plum	slim	cane

Add an Ending 1

Add *-ing* to the verbs, and write the verbs on the lines. Complete the Pattern Review.

1. hop ____________________
2. hope ____________________
3. rid ____________________
4. ride ____________________
5. tap ____________________
6. tape ____________________
7. run ____________________
8. tune ____________________

Pattern Review 2

- When adding an ending beginning with a ____________ to a 1-1-1 word, double the final __________________ before the ending.
- When adding an ending beginning with a vowel to a word ending with silent -____, drop the silent -____ before the ending.

Find the Base Form

Take off the *-ing* endings on the short-vowel and long-vowel words, and write the base form of the words on the lines. Work carefully to make the necessary changes.

1. bugging ___________
2. introducing ___________
3. closing ___________
4. bossing ___________
5. admiring ___________
6. stirring ___________
7. sniffing ___________
8. baking ___________
9. backing ___________
10. scratching ___________
11. judging ___________
12. cutting ___________
13. spilling ___________
14. ruling ___________
15. sloping ___________
16. stopping ___________

Add an Ending 2

Write the words using the indicated endings. Do not drop the silent *-e*.

1. lone + ly = ____________________
2. amuse + ment = ____________________
3. shame + less = ____________________
4. time + less = ____________________
5. same + ness = ____________________
6. wise + ly = ____________________
7. pave + ment = ____________________
8. ripe + ness = ____________________

Pattern Discovery 1

The ending *-ment* is added to a verb to change it to a ____________.

Listening Discrimination/Visual Discrimination

Pronounce these words and names with your teacher. Look at the spelling pattern in the middle of each word. Circle the words that have a short vowel in the first syllable. Complete the Pattern Review and Pattern Discovery.

1. cuter
2. cutter
3. wedding
4. Steven
5. Tommy
6. loner
7. baker
8. babble
9. pickle
10. bible
11. bugle
12. struggle
13. scraping
14. scrapping
15. scrabble
16. Bobby
17. stolen
18. chosen
19. better
20. Peter
21. sudden
22. happen
23. wafer
24. hassle
25. purist
26. plugging
27. tuner

Pattern Review 3

In a two-syllable word, a short vowel in the first syllable is almost always followed by ____ consonants or a double consonant.

Pattern Discovery 2

In a two-syllable word, a ____________ vowel in the first syllable is almost always followed by a single consonant.

❑ Remember: Short vowel + 2 consonants; long vowel + 1 consonant.

Unit 4 Review Pages

PATTERN RECAP

1. There are _____ short vowels in English.
2. In a one-syllable short-vowel word, there is usually just _____ vowel.
3. There are _____ long vowels in English.
4. Long vowels sound like the name of the ____________.
5. In a one-syllable long-vowel word, there are usually _____ vowels.
6. A common long-vowel pattern is VC__. That is, the letters _____, _____, _____, and _____ are often followed by one ___________________ and a silent _____.
7. The VC*e* pattern is not common for long _____.
8. 1-1-1 words have _____ syllable, _____ vowel, and _____ consonant at the end.
9. ____________ vowel words are never 1-1-1 words.
10. When we add an ending that begins with a vowel to a 1-1-1 word, we double the final ___________________.
11. When we add an ending that begins with a vowel to a word that ends with a silent _____, we ____________ the silent *-e*.
12. When we add an ending that begins with a consonant to a 1-1-1 word or a long-vowel word that ends with a silent -_____, we don't make any changes to the base.
13. To form the plural of some words that end in *-fe* or *-f*, we drop the -_____ or -_____ and add *-ves*.
14. When a word ends with long *o*, there are several options for forming the plural.
    - Words ending in vowel + *o* form the plural by adding -_____.
    - Musical terms ending with *-o* form the plural by adding -_____.
    - Many other words ending with consonant + *o* form the plural by adding - _____, while some form the plural by adding -_____.
    - Finally, a few words ending with consonant + *o* form the plural by adding -_____ or _____, and both plural forms are correct.
15. In two-syllable words like *pickle* or *getting*, a short vowel in the first syllable is almost always followed by _____ consonants or a double consonant.
16. In two-syllable words like *later* or *meter*, a ____________ vowel in the first syllable is almost always followed by a single consonant.

Listen and Write

Listen and write the one-syllable long-vowel words.

1. ____________ 4. ____________ 7. ____________
2. ____________ 5. ____________ 8. ____________
3. ____________ 6. ____________ 9. ____________

Choose the Best Completion

Read each sentence, and circle the word in each that best completes it. Say the words aloud, and listen for the vowel sound.

1. A hat / hate is what you wear on your head.
2. You can eat a plum / plume because it's a kind of fruit.
3. A not / note is another word for a short letter.
4. The painter wears a smock / smoke to protect her clothes.
5. When you don't want something anymore, you can get rid / ride of it.
6. If you complain about something, you grip / gripe about it.
7. Cod / Code is a kind of fish.
8. A duck / duke is a kind of bird that lives in or near the water.
9. If a snack / snake bites you, you can get very sick.
10. One square of glass in a window is a pan / pane.
11. A baby bear is a cub / cube.
12. She said that she rod / rode her bicycle to school.
13. When the workers were finished, they left a pill / pile of trash in the street.
14. When the banana is yellow, it is rip / ripe.
15. On a windy day, you can fly a kit / kite.

Find the Base Form/Ending Review

Circle the ending on each word. Tell the function of the ending and if any changes were made to the base word when the ending was added. On separate sheet of paper, write the base form of each word.

1. smoked
2. telling
3. ripeness
4. timeless
5. remotely
6. pavement
7. colonize
8. settlement
9. stopping
10. knives
11. echoes
12. widest
13. slimy
14. pianos
15. kissing
16. videos
17. wives
18. centralize

Sight Word Review

Fill in the blanks using sight words from this lesson.

1. Write your full address here: ________________________________.
2. Write the name of your school here: ________________________________.
3. Fill in the chart with the city in the left box and the state in the right box.

	Illinois
Los Angeles	
	New York
Houston	
	Florida

Add an Ending/Find the Base Form

In the middle column, write the word with the indicated ending. Then cover the left column, and write the base form in the right column. Uncover to check your work.

1. wise + ly ______ ______
2. judge + ing ______ ______
3. sun + y ______ ______
4. wife + s <u>or</u> + es ______ ______
5. care + less ______ ______
6. store + ing ______ ______
7. quick + ly ______ ______
8. hire + ed ______ ______
9. summary + ize ______ ______
10. stun + ing ______ ______
11. insure + ance ______ ______
12. radio + s <u>or</u> + es ______ ______
13. smoke + y ______ ______
14. smoke + ing ______ ______
15. tickle + ish ______ ______
16. snack + ing ______ ______
17. bake + ing ______ ______
18. tomato + s <u>or</u> + es ______ ______
19. reuse + able ______ ______
20. catch + ing ______ ______
21. sad + est ______ ______
22. modern + ize ______ ______
23. base + ment ______ ______
24. equip + ment ______ ______
25. self + s <u>or</u> + es ______ ______

26. shine + y ____________________ ____________
27. skin + y ____________________ ____________
28. cuff + s <u>or</u> + es ____________________ ____________
29. skin + less ____________________ ____________
30. decode + able ____________________ ____________
31. wrinkle + ly ____________________ ____________
32. half + s <u>or</u> + es ____________________ ____________
33. piano + s <u>or</u> + es ____________________ ____________
34. red + ish ____________________ ____________
35. state + ment ____________________ ____________

Unit 5

Long-Vowel Patterns

Unit 5 Overview

LONG-VOWEL REVIEW

Read these quotes from some famous Americans who lived in the 19th and 20th centuries, and then discuss the long-vowel words that appear in **bold** with your teacher.

Men are born to **succeed**, not **fail**.	Henry David Thoreau (1817–1862)
Always do what you are **afraid** to do.	Ralph Waldo Emerson (1803–1882)
No man **may make** another **free**.	Zora Neale Hurston (1903–1960)
I never did a **day's** work in my **life**. It was all fun.	Thomas Alva Edison (1847–1931)
When one door **closes** another door **opens**.	Alexander Graham Bell (1847–1922)
Keep your **face** to the **sunshine** and you cannot **see** the **shadow**.	Helen Keller (1880–1968)
I **grew** up **like** a **weed**—ignorant of liberty, having no experience of it.	Harriet Tubman (1820–1913)

Discuss the long-vowel words in the sayings on page 87. Identify the long vowel in each word, and count the syllables.

1. succeed	7. free	13. sunshine
2. fail	8. day's	14. see
3. always	9. life	15. shadow
4. afraid	10. closes	16. grew
5. may	11. opens	17. like
6. make	12. face	18. weed

Pattern Review 1

One-syllable long-vowel words usually have ____ vowels.

Pattern Review 2

The VC*e* pattern is a common pattern for long ____, long ____, long ____, and long ____. It is not a common pattern for long ____.

Pattern Overview

Study the chart showing the most common long-vowel patterns for each sound. C stands for consonant.

Long *a*	Long *e*	Long *i*	Long *o*	Long *u*
aCe ai ay	ee ea	iCe igh	oCe oa ow	uCe ue ew

Application

Look for other famous quotes on the Internet by searching for the people mentioned on page 87. Discuss long-vowel words in the quotes.

Lesson 21: Long *a* Patterns

Words

Pronounce these words with your teacher.

made	range	haste	rain	day
same	strange	waste	train	may
chase	change	taste	claim	play

Pattern Review 1

Long-vowel one-syllable words usually have ____ vowels. In long-vowel words, *y* and *w* are considered vowels.

Pattern Review 2

A very common long *a* pattern is -*a*C*e,* where the letter *a* is followed by ____ consonant and a silent ____.

Pattern Discovery 1

A less common long *a* pattern is -*a*CC*e,* where the letter *a* is followed by ____ consonants and a silent ____.

Pattern Discovery 2

A second very common long *a* pattern is -*ai*-, where the letters ____ are surrounded by consonants or consonant blends.

Pattern Discovery 3

When long *a* comes at the end of a syllable, the -____ pattern is most common.

Pattern Discovery 4

Pronounce these pairs of words with your teacher, and then fill in the pattern.

sale	hare	male	flare
sail	hair	mail	flair

The -*a*C*e* pattern and the -*ai*- pattern make the ____________ sound, so if the consonants are the same, then pairs of words called homophones are formed. Homophones have the____________ sound but __________________ meanings.

Listening Discrimination

Circle the words you hear.

1. chess	chase	4. fleck	flake	7. clam	claim
2. waste	west	5. stay	state	8. rang	range
3. ran	rain	6. main	men	9. pain	pen

Listen and Write 1

Write the long *a* words you hear. The words follow the -*ai*C and -*ay* patterns.

1. ____________	4. ____________	7. ____________
2. ____________	5. ____________	8. ____________
3. ____________	6. ____________	9. ____________

Listen and Write 2

Write the long *a* words you hear. The words follow the -*a*CC*e* pattern.

1. ________________	4. ________________	7. ________________
2. ________________	5. ________________	8. ________________
3. ________________	6. ________________	9. ________________

Sight Words

Study the spelling of these prepositions.

between	behind	through	toward

Choose the Best Completion

Read each sentence, and circle the word in each that best completes it. Notice the patterns in the homophones, and discuss the meanings of both words in the homophone pairs.

1. A horse has a mane / main down the back of its neck.
2. The sick man looked a little pale / pail.
3. A drink similar to beer is ale / ail.
4. You wear your belt around your waste / waist.
5. We had to climb six flights of stares / stairs.
6. I bought my new clothes when they were on sale / sail.

Listen and Write 3

Listen and fill in the preposition and the long *a* word. The long *a* words follow the *-ai*C pattern.

1. The ____________ went __________________ the tunnel.
2. The ____________ clouds are coming __________________ us.
3. We ____________ the man who was __________________ the counter.
4. The ____________ is __________________ the door and the window.

Add an Ending

Write the words using the indicated endings. Complete the Pattern Discovery.

1. stay + ed __________________
2. day + s __________________
3. pay + ment __________________
4. pray + ing __________________
5. gray + er __________________
6. way + s __________________
7. say + ing __________________
8. play + ful __________________

Pattern Discovery 5

Do not make any changes when adding __________________ to words that end with *-ay*.

Pattern Discovery 6

The ending *-ful* changes a word to an __________________.

■ Lesson 22: Long *e* Patterns

Words

Pronounce these words with your teacher.

clean	feed	peace	cheese	flea	bee	be
least	seem	please	sleeve	sea	see	he
neat	beef	leave	sneeze	tea	tree	she

Pattern Discovery 1

The most common long ____ patterns are *-ea-* and *-ee-*.

Pattern Discovery 2

Less common long ____ patterns are *-ea*C*e* and *-ee*C*e*. The only consonants that appear in the *-ea*C*e* pattern are *c,* ____, and ____. The only consonants that appear in the *-ee*C*e* pattern are ____, ____, ____, and *c* (in *fleece*).

Pattern Discovery 3

One-syllable words that end with a long *e* can end with -____, ____, or -____.

Listen and Write 1

Listen and fill in the missing consonants, then complete the Pattern Discovery.

1. __ee	5. __ee	9. __eer
2. __ea	6. __ea	10. dea__
3. sea__	7. __eat	11. pea__
4. __eem	8. mee__	12. __eek

Pattern Discovery 4

Long *e* words that follow the *-ea*C, *-ee*C, *-ea,* and *-ee* patterns form pairs of ________________. That is, they have the __________ pronunciation but ________________ meanings.

Listening Discrimination

Circle the words you hear.

1. live	leave	4. cheese	chess	7. speeds	speech
2. weave	wave	5. pitch	peach	8. each	itch
3. leak	lick	6. wheel	will	9. bet	beat

Pattern Discovery 5

After a short vowel, the sound [č] is spelled -____; after a long vowel, the sound [č] is spelled -____.

Sight Words

Study the spelling of these conjunctive adverbs.

however	otherwise	besides	nevertheless

Listen and Write 2

Write the long *e* words you hear. The words follow the -*ea*C and -*ea* patterns.

1. ____________ 4. ____________ 7. ____________
2. ____________ 5. ____________ 8. ____________
3. ____________ 6. ____________ 9. ____________

Listen and Write 3

Write the long *e* words you hear. The words follow the -*ee*C and -*ee* patterns.

1. ____________ 4. ____________ 7. ____________
2. ____________ 5. ____________ 8. ____________
3. ____________ 6. ____________ 9. ____________

Pattern Discovery 6

While the sound [k] is spelled -____ after a short vowel, it is spelled -____ after a long vowel.

Choose the Best Completion

Read each sentence, and circle the word in each that best completes it. Discuss the meanings of both words in the homophone pairs.

1. They climbed to the mountain peak / peek.
2. We called a plumber to fix the leak / leek.
3. Working two full-time jobs is a real feat / feet!
4. My dog barks every time he seas / sees the mail carrier.
5. I'd like a salad, but please don't put beats / beets in it.

Listen and Write 4

Listen and fill in the conjunctive adverb and the long *e* word. The long *e* words follow the -*ea*C*e* or -*ee*C*e* pattern.

1. She can't eat ____________; __________________, she likes yogurt.
2. We have a three year ____________; __________________, we are moving next month.
3. Be sure to ____________ a deposit for next term; __________________ you might not have a space in the class.
4. The ____________ were too short on the jacket; __________________, it was much too expensive.

Add an Ending

Write the words using the indicated endings. Complete the Pattern Discovery.

1. feel + ing __________________
2. seam + less __________________
3. read + er __________________
4. weak + ness __________________
5. green + est __________________
6. seem + ed __________________

Pattern Discovery 7

Do not make any changes when adding an ending to a __________ vowel word that follows a -VVC pattern.

■ Lesson 23: More Long *e* Patterns

Words

Pronounce these words with your teacher. Notice the long *e* sound.

piece	ceiling	goalie	donkey	baby
believe	receive	brownie	money	lucky
hygiene	deceive	calorie	key	rainy

Pattern Discovery 1

-ie- and *-ei-* both make the long *e* sound. Use *-ei-* after the letter ____. Remember this rhyme: "*i* before *e* except after *c*."

Pattern Exception

A few words that don't contain the letter *c* use -____. Some of them are *weird, either, neither,* and *leisure.*

Pattern Discovery 2

Long *e* in the last syllable of a two- or three-syllable word can be spelled -____, -____, and -____.

Listen and Write 1

Listen and fill in the final syllable. Each word ends with *-ey*.

1. jour_____
2. pars_____
3. mon_____
4. attor_____
5. ho_____
6. kid_____
7. pais_____
8. jo_____
9. chim_____

Listen and Write 2

Listen and fill in *-ie-* or *-ei-*.

1. n__ce
2. rec__pt
3. s__ge
4. perc__ve
5. c__ling
6. hyg__ne
7. p__ce
8. inconc__vable
9. rec__ver

Sight Words

Study the use of *there*, *their*, and *they're* in these examples, and use them to complete the sentences.

There is a coffee bar downstairs.

The dictionary is on the desk over **there**.

Charlie and Danny are playing with **their** toys.

They're not here right now.

1. All of the students brought ____________ books today.
2. I think the elevator is right ____________.
3. ____________ is an extra dictionary on the table.
4. ____________ busy now, so don't bother them.
5. Is anyone ____________?
6. Bonnie and Annie brought ____________ backpacks to class.

Pattern Discovery 3

Study what happens when we change these nouns to plural, and fill in the pattern.

goalie→goalies donkey→donkeys baby→babies

When a word ends with -____ or -____, we form the plural by adding *-s*. When a word ends with -____, we change the final ____ to ____ and then we add *-es*.

Add an Ending 1

Change the nouns to plural. Write the plural nouns on the lines.

1. jockey ____________________
2. city ____________________
3. calorie ____________________
4. goalie ____________________
5. chimney ____________________
6. puppy ____________________
7. kidney ____________________
8. penny ____________________

Find the Base Form

Change the nouns to singular. Write the singular form of each noun.

1. valleys ____________
2. copies ____________
3. calories ____________
4. goalies ____________
5. attorneys ____________
6. alleys ____________
7. babies ____________
8. chimneys ____________

Choose the Best Completion

Read each sentence, and circle the word in each that best completes it. Discuss the meanings of both words in the homophone pairs.

1. The hunter killed a dear / deer during hunting season.
2. I am going to meat / meet my new boss tomorrow.
3. There are seven days in a weak / week.
4. Her new shoes hurt her toes and her heal / heel.
5. I think I'll have a peace / piece of cake.
6. They stood on the peer / pier when they went fishing.

Add an Ending 2

Drop the silent *-e,* and write the indicated endings. Fill in the Pattern Review and Pattern Discovery.

1. believe + ing ________________
2. receive + er ________________
3. conceive + able ________________
4. sneeze + ed ________________
5. leave + ing ________________
6. believe + able ________________

Pattern Review

When we add an ending that begins with a __________ to a word that ends with a silent *-e*, we drop the silent ____ before adding the ending.

Pattern Discovery 4

The ending *-able* changes a verb to an ______________.

■ Lesson 24: Endings with Long *a* and Long *e*

Words

Pronounce these words with your teacher. Notice the endings.

strange	receive	rain	play	baby
stranger	receives	rainy	player	babies
strangest	receiving	raining	played	babied
strangely	receiver	rains	playing	babying
please	believe	clean	key	copy
pleasant	believes	cleaner	keying	copies
pleasure	believing	cleaning	keyed	copied
pleased	believer	cleanest	keys	copying

Pattern Review 1

When we add an ending beginning with a __________ to a word ending in a silent ____, we drop the silent ____ before adding the ending.

Pattern Review 2

When we add an ending beginning with a ______________ to a word ending in a silent ____, we keep the silent ____ when we add the ending.

Pattern Review 3

When we add endings to words following the -VVC pattern, we don't change anything before adding the ______________.

Pattern Review 4

When we add endings to words ending with *-ay* and *-ey,* we don't make any changes before adding the ______________.

Pattern Discovery

Words that end with -C*y* work this way:

To Form Plural or Third Person Singular	To Form Past Tense or Adjectives	To Form Comparative and Superlative	To Add Endings Beginning with Consonants (such as *-ly* or *-ness*)	To Add *-ing* for Progressive Verbs, Gerunds, or Adjectives
change the -*y* to -*i* and add -____	change the -*y* to -*i* and add -____	change the -*y* to -____ and add -*er* or -*est*	change the -*y* to -____ and add the ending	keep the -*y* and add -____
penny→pennies *copy→copies*	*worry→worried*	*sunny→sunnier* *pretty→prettiest*	*happy→happily* *lonely→loneliness*	*worry→worrying* *hurry→hurrying*

Sight Words

Study the spelling of these color words.

orange	blue	purple	yellow	green	brown

Sight Word Practice

Use the words in the box to complete the sentences.

1. The three primary colors are red, ____________, and ____________.
2. If you mix blue and red, it makes ____________.
3. If you mix yellow and ____________, you get green.
4. If you mix red and yellow, you get ____________.

Add an Ending 1

Change the color words by writing the words using the indicated endings.

1. If something is a little yellow, it is [yellow + ish] ________________.
2. If something is more brown, it is [brown + er] ________________.
3. If something is a little green, it is [green + ish] ________________.
4. If something is the most red, it is the [red + est] ________________.
5. If something is a little purple, it is [purple + ish] ________________.

Find the Base Form

Take off the endings, and write the base form of the long *a* and long *e* words.

1. sameness ____________
2. chasing ____________
3. cleanest ____________
4. neatly ____________
5. weakness ____________
6. bees ____________
7. strangely ____________
8. hasty ____________
9. seamless ____________
10. beefy ____________
11. peaceful ____________
12. wasteful ____________
13. tasteless ____________
14. player ____________
15. pleasant ____________
16. happily ____________
17. keys ____________
18. rainier ____________
19. journeying ____________
20. receivable ____________

Add an Ending 2

Write the words using the indicated ending or endings to each word. Pay attention to *e*-drop and words that end with *-y*.

1. taste + ful + y ________________
2. haste + y + ly ________________
3. rain + y + er ________________
4. pain + less + ly ________________
5. attorney + s ________________
6. goalie + s ________________
7. believe + able ________________
8. play + ful ________________
9. copy + ing ________________
10. please + ing + ly ________________
11. bunny + s ________________
12. study + ing ________________
13. pay + ment ________________
14. strange + ly ________________

Lesson 25: Long *o* Patterns

Words

Pronounce these words with your teacher.

rode	road	grow
joke	boat	know
home	soap	show
chose	coast	flown
whole	float	blown

Pattern Review 1

Long-vowel one-syllable words usually have ____ vowels. In long-vowel words, *y* and *w* are considered vowels.

Pattern Review 2

A very common long *o* pattern is *-oCe,* where the letter *o* is followed by ____ consonant and a silent ____.

Pattern Discovery 1

Another common long ____ pattern is *-oa-*. In this pattern, the letters ____ are surrounded by consonants or consonant blends.

Pattern Discovery 2

When long ____ appears at the end of a syllable, it is sometimes written *-ow*. Sometimes a consonant can appear after *-ow*.

Listen and Write 1

Listen and fill in the letter *a* if you hear a long *o* word.

1. bo__t	4. go__t	7. co__ch
2. co__t	5. ro__d	8. so__p
3. flo__t	6. to__st	9. mo__t

Listen and Write 2

Listen and fill in the missing letters.

1. ch__k__	4. flo__	7. co__ch
2. bo__st	5. so__k	8. sl__p__
3. co__l	6. glo__	9. sno__

Pattern Review 3

Study these pairs of words, and complete the Pattern Reviews.

catch / coach	patch / poach	scratched / approached
sack / soak	crock / croak	rocker / broker

After a short vowel, the sound [č] is spelled -____. After a long vowel, it is spelled -____.
After a short vowel, the sound [k] is spelled -____. After a long vowel, it is spelled -____.

Sight Words

Some very common sight words look like long *o* words but are pronounced differently. Pronounce these words with your teacher.

one	some	none	once

Listen and Write 3

Listen and fill in the missing words.

1. I need ____________ money. Right now I have ____________.
2. I've only been to that store ____________. I've never been to the other ____________.

Pattern Review 4

1-1-1 words have ____ syllable, ____ vowel, and ____ consonant at the end. Since *y* and *w* work like vowels in long-vowel words, words ending in -*y* and -*w* are not considered 1-1-1 words.

Visual Discrimination

Circle the words that fit the 1-1-1 pattern.

1. clock	5. boat	9. off	13. cost
2. cloak	6. Tom	10. sod	14. coast
3. spoke	7. stole	11. log	15. boast
4. clot	8. boss	12. throw	16. stop

Add an Ending 1

Write the words using the indicated endings. Pay attention to doubling and *e*-drop.

1. got + en ____________________
2. broke + en ____________________
3. Tom + y ____________________
4. soap + y ____________________
5. smoke + ing ____________________
6. rock + ing ____________________
7. quote + able ____________________
8. stop + able ____________________
9. loan + er ____________________
10. lone + er ____________________
11. nod + ed ____________________
12. toast + ed ____________________

Pattern Review

When we add an ending that begins with a vowel, we make these changes: If the word ends with silent *-e,* we ____________ the silent *e*. If we have a 1-1-1 word, we ____________ the final consonant.

Add an Ending 2

Write the words using the indicated endings for these *-o*C*y* words. Review the chart in Lesson 24 (page 99) if you can't remember how to add endings to *-y* words.

1. holy + er ____________________
2. ceremony + s ____________________
3. agony + ize ____________________
4. canopy + s ____________________
5. worry + ing ____________________
6. cozy + ly ____________________
7. nosy + est ____________________
8. rosy + ness ____________________

Unit 5 Review Pages

PATTERN RECAP

1. There are _____ long vowels in English. Long vowels sound like the name of the _____________. In a one-syllable long-vowel word, there are usually _____ vowels. The letters *y* and _____ work like vowels in long-vowel words.
2. A common long-vowel pattern is VC__. That is, the letters _____, _____, _____, and _____ are often followed by one ____________________ and a silent _____. The VC*e* pattern is not common for long ___.
3. Other common patterns for long _____ are -*a*CC*e*, -*ai*-, and -*ay*.
4. Some common patterns for long _____ are -*ea*-, -*ee*-, -*ie*-, *ei*, *ey*, and *y*.
5. Some common patterns for long _____ are -*oa*- and -*ow*-.
6. Because we have different patterns that make the same sound, we have words called ____________________. These words have the same sound but different spellings and different meanings.
7. When a word ends in -*ay*, -*ey*, or -*oy*, we do not make any changes when we add an _____________.
8. When a word ends in -C*y*, we sometimes change the *y* to *i* when we add an ending. Complete the rules in the chart.

To Form Plural or Third Person Singular	To Form Past Tense or Adjectives	To Form Comparative and Superlative	To Add Endings Beginning with Consonants (such as -*ly* or -*ness*)	To Add -*ing* for Progressive Verbs, Gerunds, or Adjectives
___ ___ ___	___ ___ ___	___ ___ ___	___ ___ ___	___ ___ ___
penny→pennies *copy→copies*	*worry→worried*	*sunny→sunnier* *pretty→prettiest*	*happy→happily* *lonely→loneliness*	*worry→worrying* *hurry→hurrying*

Rhyme

Fill in the blanks with words from the box. If you can't guess, ask your teacher or search for the rhyme on the Internet.

alone	home	know	Peep	sheep	tails

Little Bo ____________

Has lost her ____________

And doesn't ____________ where to find them.

Leave them ____________

And they'll come ____________

Wagging their ____________ behind them.

Word Builder Puzzle

Create words by selecting a consonant, consonant blend, or digraph from the first column and a vowel or vowels from the second column. Then select an optional consonant, digraph, or consonant blend from the third column, and then an optional silent *e* from the last column. How many words can you create? Many combinations are possible words. Check to see that you have made real words by asking your teacher, looking in a dictionary, or using a computer's spell-check feature. Say your words aloud to be sure they are long-vowel words and not pattern exceptions.

b, bl, br	a	*(this column is optional)*	*(this column is optional)*
cl, cr	ai		
d, dr	ay		
f, fl, fr	e	b, c, ch,	
gl, gr	ea	d, k, l,	
p, pl, pr	ee	m, n, nt,	e
s, sc, scr	ie	p, s, sh,	
sl, sn	o	st, t,	
sp, sw	oa	v, z	
st, str	ow		
squ, t, tr			

Choose the Best Completion

Read each sentence, and circle the word in each that best completes it. Notice the patterns in the homophones, and discuss the meanings of both words in the homophone pairs.

1. I got stung by a bee / be.
2. He hurt his arm yesterday and it is still sore / soar.
3. I can't here / hear you very well.
4. Vegetarians don't eat meet / meat.
5. She wore a plane / plain black dress.
6. He lives on Fourth Rode / Road.
7. Do you know how to sail / sale a boat?
8. They climbed up the stares / stairs.
9. We made / maid some mistakes on the test.
10. She cut her finger, but it will heel / heal.
11. I saw a flee / flea on my cat.
12. How much is the bus fare / fair?
13. Did someone steel / steal his car?
14. We read about some fairy tales / tails.
15. You shouldn't waist / waste paper.
16. We'll have a test next week / weak.
17. The other team beet / beat us in the tournament.
18. I got a lone / loan from the bank.

Word Knowledge

Study the quotes from page 87, and notice the words in **bold.** The words are repeated here. Tell something that you know about each word. A few have been done for you as examples.

Men are **born** to **succeed**, **not fail**.

Always do what you are **afraid** to do.

No **man may make** another **free**.

I never **did** a **day**'s **work** in my **life**. **It** was all **fun**.

When **one** door **closes** another door opens.

Keep your **face** to the **sunshine** and you cannot **see** the **shadow**.

I grew **up like** a **weed**—ignorant of liberty, having no experience of it.

Examples:

men: This is a short *e* word. It is a 1-1-1 word.

born: This is an *r*-controlled short-vowel word.

succeed: This is a two-syllable word. The first syllable has a short *u*. The second syllable has a long *e*. It follows the *-ee-* pattern.

not: This is a short *o* word. It is a 1-1-1 word.

fail: This is a long *a* word. It follows the *-ai-* pattern.

1. always
2. afraid
3. man
4. may
5. make
6. free
7. did
8. day
9. work
10. life
11. it
12. fun
13. one
14. closes
15. keep
16. face
17. sunshine
18. see
19. shadow
20. like
21. up
22. weed

Find the Base Form/Ending Review

Circle the ending on each word. Tell the function of the ending and if any changes were made to the base word when the ending was added. On separate sheet of paper, write the base form of each word.

1. badges
2. batches
3. ages
4. cuffs
5. scarves
6. ceremonies
7. plays
8. copies
9. tanning
10. taming
11. tacking
12. raging
13. bragging
14. judging
15. hurrying
16. edged
17. wedded
18. weeded
19. pianos
20. mosquitoes
21. wider
22. redder
23. happier
24. thicker
25. sunnier
26. sunny
27. happily
28. painless
29. careless
30. payment
31. pavement
32. believable
33. stoppable
34. breakable
35. freezable
36. passable

Unit 6

Long-Vowel Patterns, Long-Short Contrasts, Complex and Ambiguous Vowels

Unit 6 Overview

VOWEL REVIEW

Read these sayings with your teacher. Discuss the meaning and whether you think they are true or not. Notice the words in **bold** and write them below.

Absence makes the heart **grow** fonder.

You can't **teach** an **old** dog new **tricks**.

Time **flies** when you're having **fun**.

Work **expands** to **fill** the time you give it.

What goes **around** comes around.

Out of **sight**, out of **mind**.

You can **take** the boy out of the **country**, **but** you can't take the country out of the boy.

An **ounce** of prevention is worth a **pound** of **cure**.

Write three two-syllable words.

____________ ____________ ____________

Write three short-vowel words.

____________ ____________ ____________

Write three long-vowel words that follow a -VC*e* or -VV- pattern.

____________ ____________ ____________

Pattern Discovery 1

Most one-syllable long-vowel words have ____ vowels. However, some long-vowel words follow a -VCC or -VCCC pattern. Find three words in the sayings on page 109 that have long vowels but follow the -VCC or -VCCC pattern, and write them.

________________ ________________ ________________

Notice the sounds the vowels make in these words.

around country ounce pound

Pattern Discovery 2

These words have the same vowel sound / two vowel sounds (circle one). These sounds are called ambiguous vowels because the same two letters (____) make different sounds. They can be pronounced [au] as in *around* or *ounce,* and [ŭ] as in country.

Pronunciation Tip

Use your dictionary's pronunciation key to help you pronounce ambiguous vowels in words you don't know.

Application

Discuss sayings that you know or that you find on the Internet. Find words that follow short-vowel and long-vowel patterns.

Lesson 26: More Long *i* Patterns

Words

Pronounce these words with your teacher.

bite	night	sigh	sign	wild	kind	fly
fire	bright	high	align	child	blind	dry
line	light	thigh	assign	mild	find	cry

Pattern Exception

Most long-vowel one-syllable words have ____ vowels. However, some one-syllable long ____ words have just one vowel.

Pattern Discovery 1

A common long ____ pattern is *-ight,* and some less common long ____ patterns are *-igh, -ign, -ild,* and *-ind* (*i*CC pattern).

Pattern Discovery 2

Sometimes *-y* at the end of a word makes a long ____ sound.

Listening Discrimination

Circle the words you hear.

1.	sigh	site	4.	grind	crime	7.	bright	bride
2.	kite	kind	5.	fine	find	8.	tide	tight
3.	mild	mile	6.	chime	child	9.	blind	bribe

Visual Discrimination

Circle the 1-1-1 words.

1. sin	5. wed	9. fin
2. sign	6. weed	10. find
3. will	7. hit	11. bid
4. wild	8. high	12. blind

Pattern Extension

Some long ____ words have just one vowel, but they are never 1-1-1 words because they end with ____ or three consonants.

Listen and Write 1

Listen and fill in the missing consonants. You will write two or three consonants.

1. ri____
2. resi____
3. mi____
4. ti____
5. si____
6. chi____
7. fi____
8. si____
9. mi____

Sight Words

Study the spelling of these reflexive pronouns.

myself	yourself	himself, herself, itself
ourselves	yourselves	themselves

Pattern Review 1

To form the plural of words ending in *-f,* drop the -____ and add -____.

Listen and Write 2

Listen and fill in the reflexive pronouns and the long *i* words. The long *i* words follow the *-ight* or *-i*CC patterns.

1. I saw a picture of ____________________ as a _____________.
2. We _____________ enjoy ____________________.
3. He talked about ____________________ last _____________.
4. They congratulated ____________________ for being _____________.
5. She _____________ to ____________________.

Choose the Best Completion

Read each sentence, and circle the word in each that best completes it. Discuss the meanings of both words in the homophone pairs.

1. When she comes into the room, she always says hi / high.
2. My house is on the write / right side of the street.
3. We took a tour of the city so that we could see all of the cites / sights.
4. He said his car got scratched on the left side / sighed.
5. Please write / right your answers on another paper.
6. The judge fined / find the defendant and then sent him home.

Add an Ending

Write the words using the indicated endings, and then complete the Pattern Review.

1. might + y __________________
2. sigh + ing __________________
3. bright + ness __________________
4. child + less __________________
5. tight + er __________________
6. mild + ly __________________
7. kind + est __________________
8. thigh + s or + es __________________
9. blind + ed __________________
10. grind + er __________________

Pattern Review 2

When we add an ending to a word that follows the *-ight* or *-i*CC patterns, we do ____ make any changes to the base form.

Sight Word Practice

Write the plural form of each reflexive pronoun on the line.

1. himself __________________
2. myself __________________
3. herself __________________
4. yourself __________________

■ Lesson 27: More Long *o* Patterns

Words

Pronounce these words with your teacher.

hole	soap	roll	cold	colt	most
vote	boat	stroll	sold	bolt	host
cope	float	toll	told	jolt	ghost

Pattern Review 1

Most long-vowel one-syllable words have ____ vowels. However, some one-syllable long ____ words have just one vowel.

Pattern Discovery

A common long ____ pattern is -VCC. Examples are *-oll,* -____, -____, and *-ost.*

Listening Discrimination

Circle the words you hear.

1. coast	ghost	4. sole	sold	7. most	boast
2. troll	stroll	5. colt	coal	8. hole	hold
3. toll	told	6. bowl	bolt	9. scroll	stole

Listen and Write 1

Write the long *o* words you hear. The words follow the *-oCe* pattern.

1. ____________	4. ____________	7. ____________
2. ____________	5. ____________	8. ____________
3. ____________	6. ____________	9. ____________

Listen and Write 2

Write the long *o* words you hear. The words follow the -*o*CC pattern.

1. ____________ 4. ____________ 7. ____________
2. ____________ 5. ____________ 8. ____________
3. ____________ 6. ____________ 9. ____________

Sight Words

Study these words about family relationships.

brother	sister	grandmother	grandfather

Listen and Write 3

Listen and fill in the family relationship sight words and the long *o* words.

1. Her ________________ is ____________.
2. My ________________ ____________ me a story.
3. My ________________ isn't very ____________.
4. His ________________ has a ____________.

Choose the Best Completion

Read each sentence, and circle the word in each that best completes it. Discuss the meanings of both words in the homophone pairs.

1. The class took a pole / poll to decide which movie to watch.
2. I'd like to have my sandwich on a role / roll.
3. He bowled / bold a perfect game at the bowling alley last night.
4. Please wear soft- soled / sold shoes in the gym.
5. They road / rowed the boat on the lake.
6. That actor plays four different roles / rolls in the movie.

Find the Base Form

Take off the endings, and write the base forms of the long *i* and long *o* words.

1. nightly ________________	13. kindly ________________
2. goalposts ________________	14. scolded ________________
3. brightness ________________	15. ghosts ________________
4. sighing ________________	16. thunderbolts ________________
5. posted ________________	17. blindness ________________
6. signs ________________	18. scaffolding ________________
7. boldly ________________	19. tighter ________________
8. alignment ________________	20. mostly ________________
9. bolted ________________	21. mindful ________________
10. folding ________________	22. withholding ________________
11. assignment ________________	23. rightful ________________
12. childish ________________	24. payrolls ________________

Pattern Review 2

When we add an ending to long ____ and long ____ words that follow the -VCC or *-ight* patterns, we do ____ make any changes to the base form.

Add an Ending

Change each long *o* word to plural. Write the plural words on the lines. Review the rules in Lesson 18.

1. stereo ____________	4. taco ____________	7. echo ____________
2. potato ____________	5. hero ____________	8. radio ____________
3. piano ____________	6. zero ____________	9. tomato ____________

Lesson 28: Short-Vowel / Long-Vowel Contrasts

Words

Pronounce these words with your teacher.

dip	deep	met	mate
fit	feet	get	gate
grin	green	fed	fade
fill	feel	bled	blade
pick	peek	wreck	rake
bin	bean	bet	bait
hill	heal	pen	pain
mill	meal	men	main
lip	leap	red	raid
lick	leak	wet	wait

Pronunciation Tips

Short *i* and long *e* sound similar. Long *e* is higher and more "tense" than short *i*. Short *i* is a little lower and more "lax." Short *e* and long *a* also sound similar. Long *a* is higher and more "tense." Short *e* is a little lower and more "lax." Relax your jaw a little when you say short *i* and short *e*.

Pattern Review 1

One-syllable short-vowel words usually have ____ vowel. One-syllable long-vowel words usually have ____ vowels.

Pattern Review 2

At the end of a short-vowel syllable, we write -____ for [k] and -____ for [l], but at the end of a long-vowel syllable that contains two vowels, we write -____ for [k] and -____ for [l].

Find the Base Form

Take off the endings, and write the base form of the words on the lines. Pronounce each word to determine if the vowel is short *i*, long *e*, short *e*, or long *a*.

1. dipper ____________	5. hilly ____________	9. licks ____________
2. deeper ____________	6. healer ____________	10. leaking ____________
3. getting ____________	7. reddish ____________	11. wettest ____________
4. gates ____________	8. raided ____________	12. waiting ____________

Listening Discrimination

Listen and circle the words you hear.

1. fit	feet	4. wreck	rake	7. grin	green
2. met	mate	5. mill	meal	8. bled	blade
3. pick	peek	6. men	main	9. lip	leap

Sight Words

Study these words about family relationships.

aunt	uncle	cousin	niece	nephew

Listen and Write 1

Listen and fill in the family relationship sight words and the names. Listen carefully to decide if the name is short *e* or long *a*.

1. ____________ is my ____________.
2. My ____________ is ____________.
3. ____________ is my ____________.
4. My ____________ is ____________.
5. ____________ is my ____________.

Add an Ending

Write the words using the indicated endings. Pay attention to consonant doubling and *e*-drop.

1. fit + ness ____________
2. green + ish ____________
3. get + ing ____________
4. fade + ed ____________
5. lick + s or + es ____________
6. heal + ing ____________
7. red + est ____________
8. rake + ed ____________

Listen and Write 2

Listen and fill in with *i* or *ee*.

1. b__t
2. k__t
3. h___d
4. w__d
5. s__n
6. b__n
7. w__ck
8. str__p
9. qu__ck
10. qu__n
11. s__p
12. h__m

Listen and Write 3

Listen and fill in with *e* or *ai*.

1. w__t
2. w__t
3. g__n
4. m__n
5. m__n
6. p__l
7. f__ll
8. j__l
9. s__l
10. b__d
11. p__ck
12. s__ll

Choose and Write

Use words from the box to complete the sentences.

age	peach	peak
edge	pitch	pick

1. I had to tell them my full name and my __________.
2. In baseball, you don't throw the ball to the batter. You __________ it.
3. A nectarine is like a __________.
4. He sat on the __________ of the desk.
5. You can __________ your own strawberries.
6. It's best to get strawberries at the __________ of the season.

■ Lesson 29: Two-Syllable Words, Short/Long Contrast

Words

Pronounce these words with your teacher.

1. bet — betting
   stop — stopping
   sit — sitting
   star — starring
2. beat — beating
   sleep — sleeping
   take — taking
   stick — sticking
3. open — opening
   listen — listening
   travel — traveling
   happen — happening
4. begin — beginning
   control — controlling
   forget — forgetting
   regret — regretting

Pattern Review 1

List 1 contains 1-1-1 words. The base form has ____ syllable, ____ vowel, and ____ consonant at the end. When we add -____ to a 1-1-1 word, we double the final consonant.

Pattern Review 2

List 2 words are not 1-1-1 words. The base forms have ____ syllable, but some of these words have ____ vowels while others have ____ consonants at the end. When we add *-ing* to these words, we do ____ double the final consonant.

Pattern Discovery 1

List 3 words end with one vowel and one consonant but are not 1-1-1 words. The base forms have ____ syllables. Pronounce the base forms. The first / second (circle one) syllable has the stress. Notice that the final ________ ________ is not doubled when we add *-ing*.

Pattern Discovery 2

List 4 words end with one vowel and one consonant but are not 1-1-1 words. The base forms have ____ syllables. Pronounce the base forms. The first / second (circle one) syllable has the stress. Notice that the final consonant is doubled when we add -____.

Pattern Generalization for List 3 and List 4

When a two-syllable word has the stress on the second syllable and ends with one vowel and one consonant, then we __________ the final consonant when we add *-ing*.

Study these examples, and complete the Pattern Expansion.

forbid→forbidden rebel→rebellious admit→admitted control→controller

Pattern Expansion

The doubling rule for adding *-ing* can be extended to any ending that begins with a vowel / consonant (circle one).

Listening Discrimination

Pronounce these words with your teacher. Circle the words that have the stress on the second syllable.

1. admit	4. edit	7. omit	10. suffer
2. begin	5. collect	8. refer	11. exit
3. level	6. permit	9. forget	12. repair

Pronunciation Tip

If you can't hear the stress, look the word up in a dictionary. The stress is marked in the pronunciation guide.

Add an Ending 1

Add *-ing* to these two-syllable verbs. Write the verbs on the lines. Pay attention to consonant doubling.

1. select __________	10. resist __________
2. complain __________	11. control __________
3. refer __________	12. begin __________
4. permit __________	13. open __________
5. limit __________	14. travel __________
6. attend __________	15. occur __________
7. prefer __________	16. listen __________
8. enter __________	17. forget __________
9. prevent __________	18. happen __________

Sight Words

Study the spellings of these names of some of the joints of the human body.

elbow	wrist	knuckle	hip	knee	ankle

Choose and Write

Use words from the box for each description.

1. This two-syllable word has a short *u* and follows the -VCC + -*le* pattern.

   ____

2. This one-syllable word ends with a long *e*. ____________
3. This is a 1-1-1 word. ____________
4. This two-syllable word has a short *e* and a long *o*. ____________
5. This two-syllable word has a short *a* and follows the -VCC + -*le* pattern.

   ____

6. This one-syllable word has a short vowel but is not a 1-1-1 word. ____________

Add an Ending 2

Write the words using the indicated endings.

1. sudden + ly = ________________
2. collect + ed = ________________
3. control + er = ________________
4. sorrow + ful = ________________
5. limit + less = ________________
6. attic + s or + es = ________________
7. prevent + able = ________________
8. omit + ed = ________________
9. excel + ing = ________________
10. commit + ed = ________________

Lesson 30: Complex and Ambiguous Vowels

Words

Pronounce these words with your teacher.

boy	brown	book	thought	small	rough
toy	cow	good	bought	salt	touch
joy	crowd	foot	brought	bald	young
coin	cloud	could	caught	lawn	food
oil	found	would	taught	hawk	room
voice	count	should	pause	thaw	school

Pattern Discovery 1

The sound [oi] is written - ____ at the end of a syllable and -____ within a syllable.

Pattern Discovery 2

The sound [au] can be written two ways: -____ and - ____.

Pattern Discovery 3

The sound [ŏŏ] can be written -____ as in *book* and __________, or -____ as in *could* and __________.

Pattern Discovery 4

Four ways to write the sound [ô] are - ____ as in *thought* and __________, -____ as in *caught* and __________, *-al-* as in *salt* and __________, and -____ as in *lawn* and __________.

Pattern Discovery 5

The *-ou* in *rough* has a short ____ sound, so *rough* rhymes with *cuff.*

Pattern Discovery 6

The *-oo* in *room* has a long ____ sound, so *room* sounds like *rude.*

Pattern Discovery 7

The letter combination *-ou* has at least four pronunciations. They are [au] as in *cloud* and __________, [ŏŏ] as in *would* and __________, [ô] as in *brought* and __________, and [ŭ] (short u) as in *touch* and __________.

Listening Discrimination 1

Pronounce these pairs of words with your teacher, and decide if the words have the same vowel sound or different sounds. Write S for same and D for different.

1. crowd count _____
2. voice joy _____
3. rough could _____
4. would should _____
5. found cow _____
6. room book _____
7. good would _____
8. should bought _____
9. lawn salt _____
10. thought touch _____

Listening Discrimination 2

Listen and circle the words you hear.

1. coy coin
2. voice boys
3. crowd cloud
4. could good
5. taught thought
6. hall hawk
7. room rule
8. touch much
9. rung young
10. call caught
11. tube tooth
12. should shook

Listen and Write 1

Write the words you hear. Each word uses the ambiguous vowel *-ou*. Notice the different ways to pronounce *-ou*.

1. __________
2. __________
3. __________
4. __________
5. __________
6. __________
7. __________
8. __________
9. __________

Listen and Write 2

Write the words you hear. Each word uses the ambiguous vowel *-oo* or the complex vowel *-oi* or *-oy*. Listen for the different ways to pronounce *-oo*.

1. ____________	4. ____________	7. ____________
2. ____________	5. ____________	8. ____________
3. ____________	6. ____________	9. ____________

Sight Words

Study the spelling of these adverbs.

really	very	quite	somewhat

Listen and Write 3

Listen and fill in the blanks using sight words and words from the list on page 123.

1. My dry skin is ____________ ____________.
2. The ____________ is ________________ larger today.
3. His grandfather is ____________ ____________.
4. This ____________ is ____________ big.

Visual Discrimination

Each word on the list has the [ô] sound. Circle the vowel pattern in each word (*-ou, -au, -al,* or *-aw*). Pronounce the words with your teacher.

1. crawl	7. hawk	13. taught	19. bald
2. fault	8. tall	14. bought	20. walk
3. cough	9. ought	15. straw	21. fought
4. pause	10. sauce	16. launch	22. thaw
5. thought	11. small	17. haunt	23. wall
6. dawn	12. shawl	18. yawn	24. squawk

■ Unit 6 Review Pages

PATTERN RECAP

1. Most long-vowel one-syllable words have _____ vowels per syllable, but some long-vowel words follow a -VCC or -VCCC pattern. For example, some long _____ words are spelled with *-ight, -ign,* and *-ild,* and some long _____ words are spelled with *-oll* and *-old.*
2. At the end of a short-vowel syllable, we write -_____ for [k] and _____ for [č]. At the end of a long-vowel syllable we write -_____ for [k] and _____ for [č].
3. At the end of a short-vowel syllable, we write -_____ for [l]. At the end of a long-vowel syllable that contains two vowels, we write -_____ for [l]. Sometimes we write *-ll* after long _____ (as in *toll* or *stroll*).
4. When a two-syllable word
   - ends with one vowel and one consonant, and
   - has the stress on the second syllable

   we ____________ the final consonant before adding an ending that begins with a vowel.
5. The sounds [oi] and [au] are complex vowels. [oi] is written - _____ as in *boy* and - _____ as in *noise,* and [au] is written - _____ as in *clown* and -_____ as in *cloud.*
6. Double *o* can sound like [ŏŏ] as in ____________, or it can sound like a long ____, so *room* sounds like *rude.*
7. Four ways to write the sound [ô] are - ____ as in *thought,* -____ as in *caught,* *-al-* as in *salt,* and -____ as in *lawn.*
8. The letter combination *-ou* has several pronunciations, including [au] as in *cloud* and ____________, [ŏŏ] as in *would* and ____________, [ô] as in *brought* and ____________, and [ŭ] as in *touch* and ____________.

Choose and Write

Use long-vowel words from the box to complete the sayings.

flies	grow	makes	mind	old	teach	sight

1. Absence ____________ the heart ____________ fonder.
2. You can't ____________ an ____________ dog new tricks.
3. Out of ____________, out of ____________.
4. Time ____________ when you're having fun.

Listen and Write 1

Listen and fill in the missing consonant or consonants. Remember the patterns:

- A short vowel is followed by two or three consonants or a double consonant.
- A long vowel is followed by one consonant.

1. ke__le	7. chi__ey	13. bo__le	19. a__le
2. ri__le	8. co__ume	14. spi__al	20. du__y
3. lea__ing	9. mo__ent	15. ye__ow	21. fu__y
4. wi__ing	10. pi__ot	16. ba__y	22. e__en
5. pla__er	11. re__ent	17. cho__en	23. fa__ous
6. na__y	12. cu__ent	18. u__le	24. ca__le

Listen and Write 2

Listen and fill in the missing vowels. Listen for long and short vowels, and look at the consonant patterns.

1. __fter	7. s__lent	13. th__nder
2. h__ping	8. r__bot	14. s__ren
3. __nstant	9. f__ver	15. r__mor
4. __lbow	10. __nsect	16. l__cal
5. p__mpkin	11. w__lcome	17. s__bject
6. c__pper	12. p__ncil	18. d__ctor

Add an Ending

Write the words using the indicated endings. Pay attention to consonant doubling and *e*-drop. Use a dictionary if you cannot hear the syllable stress.

1. admit + ed = ________________
2. level + ing = ________________
3. begin + er = ________________
4. edit + ed = ________________
5. control + ing = ________________
6. settle + ment = ________________
7. purple + ish = ________________
8. forbid + en = ________________
9. suffer + ing = ________________
10. happen + ed = ________________
11. occur + ed = ________________
12. open + ing = ________________
13. listen + er = ________________
14. rebel + ious = ________________
15. commit + ment = ________________
16. commit + ed = ________________
17. travel + er = ________________
18. appear + ance = ________________
19. honest + ly = ________________
20. color + ful = ________________
21. sunny + er = ________________
22. enjoy + ed = ________________
23. study + ing = ________________
24. copy + ed = ________________

Spelling Names

Many English surnames follow common spelling patterns. Tell what you know about the spelling of these common names. How many syllables does each name have? What vowel appears in the first syllable of the two-syllable names? What consonant patterns do you see? Notice patterns of single and double consonants.

1. Smith
2. Williams
3. Brown
4. Jones
5. Miller
6. Wilson
7. Taylor
8. Martin
9. Jackson
10. White
11. Lee
12. Harris
13. Clark
14. Young
15. Green
16. Baker
17. Hill
18. Cook
19. Peters
20. Bell
21. Stevens
22. Kelly
23. Gray
24. Price
25. Russell
26. Fisher
27. James

Word Building

Many long words in English are compound words—that is, they are words made up of two or more smaller words. Combine these words to make compound words. Note that one root word can be part of several compound words, and that if you can spell the shorter words, you can spell the longer ones. All of these words have long vowels or complex or ambiguous vowels in one half or both halves.

1. down + size = ________________
2. down + stairs = ________________
3. down + town = ________________
4. count + down = ________________
5. sun + down = ________________
6. fire + house = ________________
7. fire + fight + er = ________________
8. fire + place = ________________
9. fire + proof = ________________
10. fire + wood = ________________
11. cease + fire = ________________
12. camp + fire = ________________
13. home + sick = ________________
14. home + work = ________________
15. home + made = ________________
16. life + like = ________________
17. life + time = ________________
18. life + boat = ________________
19. night + life = ________________
20. foot + hold = ________________
21. foot + stool = ________________
22. foot + note = ________________
23. foot + light + s = ________________
24. bare + foot = ________________

Listen and Write 3

Write the compound words you hear. Each syllable contains a long vowel or a complex or ambiguous vowel from Unit 6.

1. ________________
2. ________________
3. ________________
4. ________________
5. ________________
6. ________________
7. ________________
8. ________________
9. ________________
10. ________________
11. ________________
12. ________________

■ Teacher's Script

UNIT 1

Listen and Write: Unit 1 Overview (page 2)

1. hill, stick; 2. fell, then; 3. Jack, fat; 4. jump, plum; 5. Tom, Bob

Listening Discrimination 1: Lesson 1 (page 4)

1. grip 2. kick 3. slit 4. slick 5. chin 6. wit 7. spin 8. chick

Listen and Write 1: Lesson 1 (page 4)

1. bit 2. grit 3. hip 4. trip 5. chin 6. spin 7. lick 8. stick 9. slit 10. zip 11. grin 12. trick

Listen and Write 2: Lesson 1 (page 5)

1. fit 2. skip 3. tin 4. stick 5. trick 6. grin 7. slit 8. spin 9. lick

Listening Discrimination 2: Lesson 1 (page 5)

1. lit 2. tip 3. trip 4. ship 5. slip 6. sit

Listen and Write 3: Lesson 1 (page 5)

1. She bit her lip.
2. He was sick on Saturday.
3. We take a trip every weekend.
4. Did you rip the paper?
5. Don't kick the ball.

Listening Discrimination: Lesson 2 (page 7)

1. flit 2. slip 3. trip 4. chick 5. clicks 6. Rick 7. hits 8. lids

Listen and Write 1: Lesson 2 (page 7)

1. brick 2. Jim 3. big 4. mid 5. clicks 6. rims 7. pig 8. lids 9. whims

Listen and Write 2: Lesson 2 (page 8)

1. sticks 2. trips 3. slits 4. fins 5. kids 6. rims 7. tricks 8. hits 9. figs

Listen and Write: Lesson 3 (page 8)

1. Nick bought the bricks last Tuesday.
2. Click the right mouse button or hit the space bar.
3. Did the hat have a wide brim?
4. Tim put the lid on the pot to make it boil.
5. The road crews never dig on a weekday.
6. Rick will trim the bushes tomorrow.

Listening Discrimination 1: Lesson 3 (page 10)

1. scrub 2. hug 3. shrug 4. tuck 5. judge 6. truck

Listen and Write 1: Lesson 3 (page 10)

1. strut 2. shun 3. trudge 4. chuck 5. fudge 6. scrub 7. stun 8. shut 9. shrub

Listen and Write 2: Lesson 3 (page 11)

1. nut 2. fudge 3. sun 4. bum 5. budge 6. truck 7. hug 8. duck 9. pub

Listening Discrimination 2: Lesson 3 (page 11)

1. Tuesday 2. shrubs 3. trucks 4. Thursday 5. buds 6. struck

Listen and Write 3: Lesson 3 (page 11)

1. We had fun last Thursday.
2. He dug a hole in the mud in front of the little hut.
3. The truck was stuck. It wouldn't budge.
4. The shop sells dried fruit, nuts, and fudge.
5. I still have my ticket stub from the movie I saw on Wednesday.
6. They went to a pub last Tuesday.
7. That gum stuck to the bottom of my shoe.
8. If the player can't run, they'll send in a sub.

Listening Discrimination: Lesson 4 (page 13)

1. shin 2. hum 3. jig 4. hutch 5. shrub 6. dish 7. truck 8. chick

Listen and Write 1: Lesson 4 (page 13)

1. rub 2. spun 3. stick 4. mug 5. flip 6. drip 7. hutch 8. pitch 9. twist 10. rust 11. rush 12. swift

Listen and Write 2: Lesson 4 (page 14)

1. tug 2. fist 3. fig 4. chuck 5. hutch 6. tricks 7. shrubs 8. script 9. struck

Listen and Write 3: Lesson 4 (page 14)

Last year, Tim bought a big truck. It was six years old, but it was in good condition. It had a hitch on the back so he could pull his boat. Now Tim is having some bad luck with his truck. First, he had to replace the clutch because he couldn't shift the gears. Then the truck got stuck in some mud and a hub cap fell off the wheel. Last night, someone hit the truck in a parking lot. Now Tim wonders what is going to happen next.

Listen and Write 1: Lesson 5 (page 16)

1. fridge 2. cliff 3. bliss 4. fluff 5. twig 6. budge 7. puff 8. hiss 9. bridge 10. hull 11. stiff 12. judge

Listen and Write 2: Lesson 5 (page 16)

1. dig 2. plug 3. grudge 4. cliff 5. puff 6. bridge 7. gull 8. miss

Listen and Write 3: Lesson 5 (page 17)

1. kiss 2. hull 3. stiff 4. budge 5. dig 6. bridge 7. plug 8. truss 9. bill

Listen and Write 1: Unit 1 Review (page 19)

1. pit 2. cut 3. tin 4. rig 5. stuck 6. sick 7. grudge 8. ridge 9. strut 10. pitch 11. crutch 12. much 13. rich 14. cliff 15. miss 16. cuff 17. pill 18. fuss 19. gull 20. bridge 21. Dutch 22. trick 23. judge 24. ditch

Listen and Write 2: Unit 1 Review (page 20)

Rose had a busy week. On Monday, she went grocery shopping. Her fridge was empty and she needed to fill it up. On Tuesday, Rose had an appointment with her hairdresser, Kim. Rose wanted Kim to cut her hair. Kim did a good job. On Wednesday, Rose took a little trip. She visited her brother Tim. Tim had been sick, but he was feeling better. Rose gave Tim a hug and a kiss before she left his house. Tim doesn't like it when Rose makes a fuss over him. On Thursday, Rose worked in her yard. She had to dig a little ditch at the edge of the garden, trim the shrubs, and pick up some stuff that blew over in a storm. Today is Friday. Rose is going to run some errands today. She is hoping to get some rest on the weekend.

UNIT 2

Listen and Write 1: Lesson 6 (page 25)

1. lash 2. latch 3. mass 4. match 5. patch 6. pack 7. pass 8. trash 9. track 10. splash 11. brass 12. scratch

Listen and Write 2: Lesson 6 (page 26)

1. pats 2. rack 3. bags 4. scrap 5. latch 6. masks 7. thanks 8. dash

Listening Discrimination 2: Lesson 6 (page 26)

1. pack 2. tuck 3. miss 4. hutch 5. clack 6. hash

Listen and Write 3: Lesson 6 (page 26)

1. cuff 2. class 3. stiff 4. rich 5. clutch 6. catch 7. brush 8. stitch

Listen and Write 1: Lesson 7 (page 27)

1. clock 2. dodge 3. scotch 4. doll 5. blob 6. prod 7. crop 8. fog 9. Tom 10. Ron 11. honk 12. block

Listen and Write 2: Lesson 7 (page 29)

1. seven bridges 2. twelve classes 3. nine stitches 4. eight bushes 5. eleven lodges 6. eight judges

Listen and Write 3: Lesson 7 (page 29)

1. tacks 2. jobs 3. rashes 4. blocks 5. patches 6. passes 7. drops 8. spots

Listen and Write 1: Lesson 8 (page 32)

1. fret 2. then 3. fleck 4. pest 5. trend 6. wreck 7. shed 8. blend 9. chest

Listen and Write 2: Lesson 8 (page 32)

1. spent 2. pegs 3. neck 4. nests 5. bled 6. hen 7. bets 8. west 9. went

Listen and Write 3: Lesson 8 (page 32)

I put five short *e* words in alphabetical order. The first word is blend. The second word is crest. The third word is fleck. The fourth word is mend. And the fifth word is vest.

Listening Discrimination: Lesson 9 (page 34)

1. set 2. bomb 3. etches 4. knacks 5. masses 6. bends

Listen and Write 1: Lesson 9 (page 34)
1. smells 2. wedges 3. blotches 4. badges 5. dresses 6. smocks 7. scratches 8. jobs 9. passes 10. staffs 11. flecks 12. crests

Listen and Write 2: Lesson 9 (page 35)
1. fifteen wedges 2. thirteen tracks 3. sixteen jets 4. fourteen clocks 5. thirteen dresses 6. sixteen scratches

Listening Discrimination 1: Lesson 10 (page 37)
1. forty 2. hurt 3. fur 4. burst 5. cart 6. church

Listening Discrimination 2: Lesson 10 (page 37)
1. hurt 2. fun 3. stern 4. bust 5. Kirk 6. bud

Listen and Write: Lesson 10 (page 38)
1. birth 2. church 3. third 4. harm 5. snarl 6. worth 7. born 8. Thursday 9. torch

Listen and Write: Unit 2 Review (page 40)
1. Bond 2. strap 3. sketch 4. lark 5. blink 6. burn 7. brim 8. blond 9. lump 10. skid 11. strum 12. ban

UNIT 3

Listen and Write 1: Lesson 12 (page 48)
1. stick 2. squish 3. fast 4. quick 5. trick 6. shut 7. squint 8. quack 9. squat

Listen and Write 2: Lesson 1 (page 50)
1. Ed went hunting last July.
2. Bobby went fishing last June.
3. Sally went jogging last August.
4. Tom went running last May.

Listen and Write 3: Lesson 12 (page 50)
1. flipping 2. better 3. curly 4. happy 5. quickest 6. faster

Listen and Write 1: Lesson 13 (page 52)
1. chuckle 2. crinkle 3. fiddle 4. raffle 5. dabble 6. jiggle 7. hassle 8. jungle 9. dimple

Listen and Write 2: Lesson 13 (page 52)
1. riddle 2. muddle 3. jiggle 4. kettle 5. hassle 6. bobble 7. little 8. struggle 9. goggle

Listen and Write 3: Lesson 13 (page 52)
1. They held a raffle last December.
2. Fall begins in the middle of September.
3. They pick apples in October.
4. The weather in November is a little cool.

Listen and Write 4: Lesson 13 (page 52)

1. apple 2. buckle 3. cripple 4. drizzle 5. freckle 6. guzzle 7. hassle 8. jingle 9. little 10. muddle 11. nettle 12. paddle 13. quibble 14. riddle 15. snuggle 16. tickle 17. uncle 18. waffle

Listen and Write 1: Lesson 14 (page 55)

1. hit 2. slant 3. wick 4. spun 5. clicks 6. jobs 7. scrub 8. badge 9. clutch 10. tricks 11. cliff 12. fuss 13. hills 14. splash 15. match 16. press 17. drop 18. smack 19. nest 20. rents 21. plot

Listen and Write 2: Lesson 14 (page 56)

1. happen 2. witness 3. center 4. market 5. member 6. sudden 7. winter 8. gossip 9. sister

Listen and Write 3: Lesson 15 (page 59)

1. help 2. helps 3. helper 4. helpless 5. skin 6. skinny 7. skinless 8. skins 9. stiff 10. stiffer 11. stiffness 12. stiffly 13. dull 14. dullness 15. track 16. trackless 17. tracks 18. tracker

UNIT 4

Listening Discrimination: Lesson 16 (page 67)

1. tap 2. plane 3. fate 4. rake 5. van 6. hat 7. mad 8. shake 9. staff

Listen and Write: Lesson 16 (page 68)

1. grade 2. scrap 3. pan 4. came 5. slat 6. dame 7. shade 8. cap 9. shame

Listening Discrimination: Lesson 17 (page 70)

1. rod 2. like 3. tame 4. slim 5. kite 6. don

Listen and Write 1: Lesson 17 (page 70)

1. fire 2. rip 3. fin 4. slime 5. ride 6. bribe 7. dim 8. win 9. site

Listen and Write 2: Lesson 17 (page 71)

1. describe 2. advice 3. beside 4. turnpike 5. exile 6. admire 7. advise 8. surprise 9. device

Listen and Write 1: Lesson 18 (page 74)

1. rob 2. code 3. tom 4. tone 5. hope 6. note 7. cop 8. rod 9. lobe

Listen and Write 2: Lesson 18 (page 74)

1. The building is on New York Avenue.
2. She lives on North Ode Street.
3. The school is on Third Avenue.
4. She lives on Fourth Road.
5. It is near West Side Highway.

Listen and Write 1: Lesson 19 (page 77)

1. rude 2. hug 3. plum 4. tune 5. us 6. brute 7. cub 8. cute 9. tube

Listen and Write 2: Lesson 19 (page 77)

1. parachute 2. produce 3. refuse 4. include 5. insure 6. execute 7. amuse 8. reduce 9. excuse

Listen and Write: Lesson 20 (page 79)

1. chose 2. rule 3. fine 4. alone 5. quake 6. swipe 7. brute 8. stroke 9. amuse 10. wine 11. rate 12. crude

Listen and Write: Unit 4 Review (page 83)

1. rude 2. spine 3. quite 4. rose 5. bake 6. race 7. spoke 8. vote 9. cube

UNIT 5

Listening Discrimination: Lesson 21 (page 90)

1. chase 2. west 3. rain 4. fleck 5. stay 6. main 7. claim 8. rang 9. pen

Listen and Write 1: Lesson 21 (page 90)

1. gray 2. brain 3. pail 4. stray 5. faith 6. play 7. jay 8. grain 9. trail

Listen and Write 2: Lesson 21 (page 90)

1. change 2. waste 3. range 4. strange 5. haste 6. exchange 7. taste 8. arrange 9. paste

Listen and Write 3: Lesson 21 (page 91)

1. The train went through the tunnel.
2. The rain clouds are coming toward us.
3. We paid the man who was behind the counter.
4. The painting is between the door and the window.

Listen and Write 1: Lesson 22 (page 92)

1. see 2. sea 3. seam 4. seem 5. flee 6. flea 7. meat 8. meet 9. deer 10. dear 11. peak 12. peek

Listening Discrimination: Lesson 22 (page 93)

1. live 2. weave 3. lick 4. chess 5. pitch 6. wheel 7. speeds 8. each 9. beat

Listen and Write 2: Lesson 22 (page 93)

1. tea 2. clean 3. bead 4. sea 5. lead 6. scream 7. weak 8. peach 9. stream

Listen and Write 3: Lesson 22 (page 93)

1. beep 2. bleed 3. three 4. queen 5. peep 6. bee 7. sleek 8. speech 9. street

Listen and Write 4: Lesson 22 (page 94)

1. She can't eat cheese; however, she likes yogurt.
2. We have a three year lease; nevertheless, we are moving next month.
3. Be sure to leave a deposit for next term; otherwise you might not have a space in the class.
4. The sleeves were too short on the jacket; besides, it was much too expensive.

Listen and Write 1: Lesson 23 (page 95)

1. journey 2. parsley 3. monkey 4. attorney 5. hockey 6. kidney 7. paisley 8. jockey 9. chimney

Listen and Write 2: Lesson 23 (page 95)

1. niece 2. receipt 3. siege 4. perceive 5. ceiling 6. hygiene 7. piece 8. inconceivable 9. receiver

Listen and Write 1: Lesson 25 (page 101)

1. boat 2. cot 3. float 4. got 5. rod 6. toast 7. coach 8. sop 9. moat

Listen and Write 2: Lesson 25 (page 102)

1. choke 2. boast 3. coal 4. flow 5. soak 6. glow 7. coach 8. slope 9. snow

Listen and Write 3: Lesson 25 (page 102)

1. I need some money. Right now I have none.
2. I've only been to that store once. I've never been to the other one.

UNIT 6

Listening Discrimination: Lesson 26 (page 111)

1. sigh 2. kite 3. mile 4. grind 5. fine 6. child 7. bright 8. tide 9. blind

Listen and Write 1: Lesson 26 (page 112)

1. right 2. resign 3. mild 4. tight 5. sigh 6. child 7. fight 8. sign 9. might

Listen and Write 2: Lesson 26 (page 112)

1. I saw a picture of myself as a child.
2. We might enjoy ourselves.
3. He talked about himself last night.
4. They congratulated themselves for being right.
5. She sighs to herself.

Listening Discrimination: Lesson 27 (page 114)

1. ghost 2. stroll 3. told 4. sole 5. coal 6. bowl 7. most 8. hold 9. stole

Listen and Write 1: Lesson 27 (page 114)

1. rope 2. woke 3. close 4. stone 5. broke 6. hole 7. phone 8. joke 9. note

Listen and Write 2: Lesson 27 (page 115)

1. most 2. jolt 3. fold 4. roll 5. host 6. bolt 7. hold 8. stroll 9. post

Listen and Write 3: Lesson 27 (page 115)

1. Her sister is Rose.
2. My grandfather told me a story.
3. My brother isn't very old.
4. His grandmother has a cold.

Listening Discrimination: Lesson 28 (page 118)

1. fit 2. mate 3. peek 4. wreck 5. mill 6. main 7. green 8. bled 9. lip

Listen and Write 1: Lesson 28 (page 118)

1. Tess is my aunt.
2. My cousin is Ben.
3. Nate is my uncle.
4. My niece is Kate.
5. Ken is my nephew.

Listen and Write 2: Lesson 28 (page 119)

1. beet 2. kit 3. hid 4. weed 5. seen 6. bin 7. wick 8. strip 9. quick 10. queen 11. seep 12. him

Listen and Write 3: Lesson 28 (page 119)

1. wait 2. wet 3. gain 4. main 5. men 6. pail 7. fell 8. jail 9. sail 10. bed 11. peck 12. sell

Listening Discrimination 2: Lesson 30 (page 124)

1. coin 2. voice 3. crowd 4. good 5. taught 6. hawk 7. room 8. touch 9. rung 10. caught 11. tube 12. should

Listen and Write 1: Lesson 30 (page 124)

1. ground 2. should 3. brought 4. touch 5. found 6. bought 7. could 8. young 9. count

Listen and Write 2: Lesson 30 (page 125)

1. coin 2. book 3. food 4. boy 5. room 6. good 7. noise 8. school 9. foot

Listen and Write 3: Lesson 30 (page 125)

1. My dry skin is quite rough.
2. The crowd is somewhat larger today.
3. His grandfather is very bald.
4. This school is really big.

Listen and Write 1: Unit 6 Review (page 127)

1. kettle 2. rifle 3. leaning 4. winning 5. planner 6. navy 7. chimney 8. costume 9. moment 10. pilot 11. recent 12. current 13. bottle 14. spiral 15. yellow 16. baby 17. chosen 18. uncle 19. ankle 20. duty 21. funny 22. even 23. famous 24. candle

Listen and Write 2: Unit 6 Review (page 127)

1. after 2. hoping 3. instant 4. elbow 5. pumpkin 6. copper 7. silent 8. robot 9. fever 10. insect 11. welcome 12. pencil 13. thunder 14. siren 15. rumor 16. local 17. subject 18. doctor

Listen and Write 3: Unit 6 Review (page 129)

1. seafood 2. railroad 3. daylight 4. greenhouse 5. houseboat 6. playmate 7. hideout 8. outlook 9. nightmare 10. childhood 11. bookcase 12. wildlife